KASHMIR

KASHMIR

The Case for Freedom

Tariq Ali
Hilal Bhatt
Angana P. Chatterji
Habbah Khatun
Pankaj Mishra
Arundhati Roy

VERSO
London • New York

First published by Verso 2011
The collection © Verso 2011
Individual contributions © the contributors

All rights reserved

3 5 7 10 8 6 4 2

Verso
UK: 6 Meard Street, London W1F 0EG
US: 20 Jay Street, Suite 1010, Brooklyn, NY 11201
www.versobooks.com

Verso is the imprint of New Left Books

ISBN-13: 978-1-84467-735-1

British Library Cataloguing in Publication Data
A catalogue record for this book is available from the British Library

Library of Congress Cataloguing-in-Publication Data
A catalog record for this book is available from the Library of Congress

Typeset in Fournier by Hewer Text UK Ltd, Edinburgh
Printed in the USA

Contents

Chronology: 1947–2010   vii

Introduction   1
  by Pankaj Mishra

The Story of Kashmir   7
  by Tariq Ali
Azadi: The Only Thing Kashmiris Want   57
  by Arundhati Roy
Poems by a Queen of Kashmir   72
  by Habbah Khatun
Fayazabad 31223   78
  by Hilal Bhatt
The Militarized Zone   93
  by Angana P. Chatterji
Seditious Nehru   125
  by Arundhati Roy

Afterword: Not Crushed, Merely Ignored   132
  by Tariq Ali
About the Authors   139

Chronology: 1947–2010

15 August 1947: British India is partitioned into the independent nation-states of India and Pakistan. The rulers of 'princely states', bearing in mind the wishes of their people, are to choose whether to accede to India or Pakistan. The Maharaja Hari Singh, Hindu ruler of Muslim-majority Kashmir, delays his decision.

October 1947: Armed tribesmen from Pakistan's North-West Frontier Province enter Kashmir to join an internal revolt in the Poonch region. The tribesmen go on the rampage, looting and raping locals.

26 October 1947: Requesting help from India in quelling the revolt and invasion, the Maharaja signs the Instrument of Accession, acceding Kashmir to India. The accession is seen as provisional pending a plebiscite to determine the will of the Kashmiri people.

27 October 1947: Indian forces are airlifted into Srinagar to repel the Pakistani militias. The fighting escalates into the first Indo-Pakistan war, with Pakistan disputing the accession and eventually sending in regular forces.

1 January 1948: India formally refers the Kashmir situation to the United Nations.

5 February 1948: A UN resolution calls for an immediate cease-fire and a plebiscite.

1 January 1949: The UN-brokered cease-fire ends the first Indo-Pakistan war, with India and Pakistan agreeing to a plebiscite and the withdrawal of troops behind the cease-fire line, leaving two-thirds of Kashmir under Indian control.

26 January 1950: The constitution of India comes into effect. Article 370 accords autonomous status to Jammu and Kashmir, with Indian jurisdiction restricted to defence, foreign affairs and communications.

October 1950: The National Conference party, led by Sheikh Abudullah, calls for elections in Jammu and Kashmir to create a constituent assembly to determine the future of Kashmir.

30 March 1951: A UN Security Council resolution rejects elections as a substitute for a plebiscite to determine the future status of Kashmir and appoints a representative to effect demilitarization, which is unsuccessful.

September 1951: Amid allegations of vote rigging, National Conference wins all seventy-five seats unopposed in Constituent Assembly elections.

31 October 1951: In his first speech to the assembly, Sheikh Abdullah argues for accession to India.

July 1952: Sheikh Abdullah signs the Delhi Agreement, providing for autonomy for Jammu and Kashmir within India.

July 1953: The development of the Prasad protest movement (led by Syama Prasad Mookerjee) in 1952, calling for the complete accession and integration of Kashmir into India, pushes Abdullah to make proposals for independence.

8 August 1953: Abdullah is dismissed as prime minister and arrested and imprisoned by India. Bhashi Ghulam Mohammad takes his place. Protests are put down with force.

17–20 August 1953: Indian and Pakistani prime ministers meet in New Delhi and agree to the appointment of a plebiscite administrator by the end of April 1954. However, as the alliance between Pakistan and the US deepens, Indian considerations over Kashmir become coloured by the Cold War and the plebiscite is off the table.

February 1954: The Constituent Assembly ratifies the accession to India.

14 May 1954: The Constitution (Applicable to Jammu and Kashmir) Order, 1954 comes into force, extending Indian jurisdiction over Kashmir, effectively annulling the Delhi Agreement and curbing civil liberties.

24 January 1957: The UN Security Council reaffirms its 1951 resolution, stating that no action taken by the Constituent Assembly can be a substitute for a plebiscite in determining the final disposition of the state.

26 January 1957: The Constituent Assembly enacts the Constitution of Jammu and Kashmir, which states that 'the State of Jammu and Kashmir is and shall be an integral part of the Union of India'.

9 August 1955: The Plebiscite Front is established to press for Sheikh Abdullah's release and a plebiscite under UN auspices to decide the future of Kashmir.

20 October–20 November 1962: A border dispute in the Ladakh region sparks war between India and China, resulting in territorial gains for China from both India and Pakistan.

March 1965: The Indian Parliament passes a bill declaring Kashmir a province of India, claiming for India the power to appoint a governor, dismiss Kashmir's government and assume its legislative functions.

August–23 September 1965: The second Indo-Pakistan war over Kashmir breaks out after Pakistan sends armed infiltrators across the 1949 cease-fire line.

10 January 1966: India and Pakistan sign the Tashkent Declaration, agreeing to pull back to pre-1965 positions.

3–16 December 1971: The Indo-Pakistan war results in Indian victory and the succession of East Pakistan as the independent state of Bangladesh.

February 1972: The Plebiscite Front is banned from participating in the State Assembly election.

2 July 1972: India and Pakistan sign the Simla Agreement, which redesignates the UN cease-fire line in Kashmir as the 'Line of Control', to be respected by both parties, who are to resolve the Kashmir dispute through bilateral talks.

13 November 1974: In return for Sheikh Abdullah's release and reinstatement as chief minister of Jammu and Kashmir, his deputy, Mirzal Afza Beg, signs an accord reiterating the State of Jammu and Kashmir as a constituent unit of India, without the condition for pre-1953 autonomy.

23 May 1977: Abdullah threatens succession unless India respects the provisions of Article 370 regarding Kashmir's autonomy.

8 September 1982: Sheikh Abdullah dies. His son, Farooq Abdullah, assumes his position.

June 1984: Ghulam Mohammad Shah and other National Conference assembly members defect to form a new government. Jagmohan, the New Delhi–appointed governor of Jammu and Kashmir and a Hindu nationalist, dismisses Farooq Abdullah; Shah is appointed chief minister. Protests erupt and Shah imposes extended curfews.

7 March 1986: The Shah is dismissed from his post and Jagmohan assumes exclusive power, which he uses to restrict the government employment of Muslims.

23 March 1987: The vastly popular Muslim United Front (MUF) contests the 1987 State Assembly elections. The

Congress–Conference Alliance wins amid widespread allegations of poll rigging. Fierce repression thwarts any mass uprising against Farooq Abdullah's unpopular reinstated government.

1989: Armed resistance to Indian rule breaks out, spearheaded by formerly imprisoned MUF members. Strikes take up one-third of the year's working days and the State Assembly election is boycotted – turnout is under 5 per cent.

1990s: The insurgency continues; Pakistan-sponsored militant Islamic groups proliferate and Indian militarization intensifies.

20 January 1990: The day after Jagmohan is reappointed governor of Kashmir, the Indian paramilitary Central Reserve Police Force (CRPF) fires on a group of unarmed demonstrators, including women and children, in Gawkadal. The Gawkadal massacre prompts the mass demonstrations of hundreds of thousands, which are met with further violence.

1 March 1990: More than half a million people march to the offices of the UN Military Observer Group in Srinagar to demand the implementation of UN resolutions stressing the importance of the plebiscite and self-determination. The Indian army fires on demonstrators, killing twenty-six civilians at Zakoora Crossing and twenty-one at the Tengpora bypass.

30 March 1990: The largest political rally in Kashmir yet at the funeral of Ashfaq Wani, Jammu and Kashmir Liberation Front leader.

6 January 1993: The Sopore Massacre – Indian Border Security Police kill at least fifty-five unarmed civilians in Sopore in revenge for a militant ambush on one of their security patrols.

March 1993: Political, social and religious groups form the All Party Hurriyat Conference ('Hurriyat' meaning freedom in Urdu), calling for self-determination.

21 February 1999: Indian prime minister Atal Bihari Vajpayee and Pakistani prime minister Nawaz Sharif sign the Lahore Declaration, which focused on, among other issues, peaceful resolution of the Kashmir problem.

May–July 1999: The Kargil War, fought by India and Pakistan in the Kargil district of Kashmir.

2000s: The decade sees the armed struggle yield to a new phase of mass, non-violent protest. India and Pakistan restore diplomatic ties – engaging in talks over Kashmir and implementing confidence building measures – although this is interrupted sporadically by incidents of violence. The Indo-Pakistan diplomacy does not result in demilitarization in Kashmir or any agreement on its future.

May 2008: The decision by the Government of India and the state Government of Jammu and Kashmir to transfer land to the Hindu Shri Amarnath Shrine Board sparks the most widespread and sustained mass uprising against Indian rule since 1990. Armed police fire on the protesters, and the only functional road between Kashmir and India is blockaded.

21 February 2009: The Bomai killings, in which two worshippers were shot when the Indian army fired indiscriminately, inflames large protests in Bomai and surrounding districts, which then face indefinite curfew.

29–30 May 2009: Two women, Neeolfar Jan, twenty-two, and Asiya Jan, seventeen, are gang-raped and murdered in the Shopian district of India-administered Kashmir.

June 2009: Large protests erupt across the Kashmir Valley, accusing the CPRF of the rapes and murders. The protests are met with force and an undeclared curfew is imposed on the Shopian district.

30 April 2010: The Indian army claims to have killed three armed infiltrators crossing the Line of Control in the Machil Sector. It is later found that the encounter was staged and that the dead three were Kashmiri civilians, shot so that their killers could claim a cash reward.

11 June 2010: Tufail Ahmad Mattoo, seventeen, is struck in the head and killed by a teargas canister fired at close range, while walking home from school. His death sets off another summer of protest, during which a military curfew is imposed and more than a hundred Kashmiris are killed.

Pankaj Mishra

Introduction

Once known for its extraordinary beauty, the valley of Kashmir now hosts the biggest, bloodiest and also most obscure military occupation in the world. With more than eighty thousand people dead in an anti-India insurgency backed by Pakistan, the killing fields of Kashmir dwarf those of Palestine and Tibet. In addition to the everyday regime of arbitrary arrests, curfews, raids, and checkpoints enforced by nearly 700,000 Indian soldiers, the valley's four million Muslims are exposed to extrajudicial execution, rape, and torture, with such barbaric variations as live electric wires inserted into penises.

Why, then, does the immense human suffering of Kashmir occupy such an imperceptible place in our moral imagination? After all, the Kashmiris demanding release from the degradations of military rule couldn't be louder or clearer. India has contained the insurgency of 1989, which it provoked with rigged elections and massacres of protestors. The hundreds of thousands of demonstrators who periodically fill the streets of Kashmir's cities today are overwhelmingly young, many in their teens, and armed with nothing more lethal than stones. Yet the Indian state seems determined to strangle the voices of the new generation as it did those of the old one. In the summer of 2010, soldiers shot dead more than a hundred protesters, most of them teenagers.

The *New York Times* described these protests as a comprehensive 'intifada-like popular revolt'. They have a broader mass base than the Green Movement does in Iran, or indeed than the uprisings in the Arab world have enjoyed. But no colour-coded revolution is heralded in Kashmir by Western commentators. BBC and CNN don't endlessly loop clips of little children being shot in the head by Indian soldiers. Bloggers and tweeters in the West fail to keep virtual vigils by the side of the dead and the wounded. The United Nations does not hold emergency sessions to discuss its response to the killing of scores of unarmed protestors.

Kashmiri Muslims are understandably bitter. As Parvaiz Bukhari, a journalist, says, the stones flung randomly by protesters have become the expression of a 'neglected people' convinced that the world deliberately ignores their plight. The veteran Kashmiri journalist Masood Hussain confesses to the near-total futility of his painstaking auditing of atrocity over two decades. For Kashmir has turned out to be a 'great suppression story'.

The cautiousness – or timidity – of Western politicians is easy to understand. Apart from appearing a lifeline to flailing Western economies, India is a counterweight to China, at least in the fantasies of Western strategists. A month before his election, Barack Obama declared that resolving the 'Kashmir crisis' was among his 'critical tasks'. Since then, Obama hasn't uttered a word about this *ur*-crisis that has seeded all major conflicts in South Asia. David Cameron was advised to maintain a similar strategic public silence during his visit to India last year.

Those Western pundits who are always ready to assault illiberal regimes worldwide on behalf of democracy ought not to be so tongue-tied. Here is a well-educated Muslim population, heterodox and pluralist by tradition and temperament, and desperate for genuine democracy. However, intellectuals preoccupied by transcendent, nearly mystical, battles between civilization and barbarism tend to assume that 'democratic' India, a natural ally of the 'liberal' West, must be doing the right thing in Kashmir, that is, fighting 'Islamofascism'. Thus Christopher Hitchens could call upon the Bush administration to establish a military alliance with 'the other great multiethnic democracy under attack from Muslim fascism', even as an elected Hindu nationalist government stood accused of organizing a pogrom that killed more than two thousand Muslims in the Indian state of Gujarat.

Electoral democracy in multiethnic, multireligious India is one of the modern era's most utopian political experiments, increasingly vulnerable to malfunction and failure and, consequently, to militant disaffection and state terror. But then the West's new masters of humanitarian war, busy painting grand ideological struggles on broad, rolling canvases, are prone to miss the human position of suffering and injustice.

Indian writers and intellectuals, who witnessed the hijacking of India's secular democracy by Hindu supremacists, seem better acquainted with the messy realities concealed by stirring abstractions. But on Kashmir they often appear as evasive as their Chinese peers are on Tibet.

People in mass democracies are usually slow to recognize the nature of the undeclared wars conducted by their representatives. But by the late 1960s there was hardly a public figure in the United States – from J.K. Galbraith to Philip Roth – who did not feel compelled to build up a chorus of denunciation against the country's deeply dishonourable involvement in Indochina. In comparison, the deaths, in less than two decades, of nearly eighty thousand people in neighbouring Kashmir have barely registered in the Indian liberal conscience.

Indians may have justifiably recoiled from the fundamentalist and brutish aspect of the revolt in the valley. But the massive non-violent protests in Kashmir since 2008 have hardly released a flood of pent-up sympathy from them.

A few Indian commentators have deplored, consistently and eloquently, India's record of rigged elections and atrocity in the valley, even if they speak mainly in terms of defusing rather than heeding Kashmiri aspirations. But many more have tended to become nervous at the mention of disaffection in the Kashmir Valley. 'I am not taking up that thorny question here', Amartya Sen writes in a footnote devoted to Kashmir in *The Argumentative Indian*. In the more resonant context of a book titled *Identity and Violence*, Sen yet again relegates the subject to a footnote.

A commonplace secular-nationalist argument in India is that Kashmiri Muslims, if given the slightest concessions by India, would go radically Islamist or embrace Pakistan, emboldening separatists in the northeast. But it has never been clear that radical Islam has a sustainable appeal in Kashmir. The Kashmiri feeling for Pakistan, too, is highly capricious, almost entirely fuelled by hatred of the Indian military occupation.

Certainly, as Arundhati Roy's near-imprisonment for 'sedition' proves, anyone initiating a frank discussion of Kashmir in India risks not only the malevolence of Hindu nationalists but also a storm of vituperation from the Indian understudies of Bill O'Reilly and Sean Hannity. The choleric TV anchors, partisan journalists, and opinion-mongers of India's corporate media routinely amplify the falsehoods and deceptions of Indian intelligence agencies in Kashmir. Blaming Pakistan or

Islamic fundamentalists, as *The Economist* pointed out after massive peaceful demonstrations in Kashmir in 2010, has 'got much harder' for the Indian government, which has 'long denied the great extent to which Kashmiris want rid of India.' Nevertheless, it tries, and as the political philosopher Pratap Bhanu Mehta, one of the few fair-minded commentators on this subject, points out, the Indian media now acts in concert with the government 'to deny any legitimacy to protests in Kashmir.'

This effective censorship reassures those Indians anxious not to let mutinous Kashmiris sully the currently garish notions of India as an 'economic powerhouse' and 'vibrant democracy' — the calling cards with which Indian elites apply for membership in the exclusive clubs of the West. In Kashmir, however, the net effect is deeper anger and alienation. As Parvaiz Bukhari puts it, Kashmiris hold India's journalists, as much as its politicians, responsible for 'muzzling and misinterpreting' them.

'The promise of a liberal India', Mehta writes, 'is slowly dying.' For Kashmiris, this promise has proved as hollow as that of the fundamentalist Islam exported by Pakistan. Liberated from political deceptions, the young men on the streets of Kashmir today seem simply to want to express their hatred of the state's impersonal brutality and to commemorate lives freshly ruined by it. As the Kashmiri writer Basharat Peer wrote in his moving 'Letter to an Unknown Indian', Indian journalists might edit out the 'faces of the murdered boys' and 'their grieving fathers', they may not show 'the video of a woman in Anantnag, washing the blood of the boys who were killed outside her house', but 'Kashmir sees the unedited Kashmir.'

And it remembers. 'Like many other Kashmiris,' Peer writes, 'I have been in silence, committing to memory the deed, the date.' Apart from the youth on the streets, there are also those with their noses in books, or pressed against window bars. Soon this generation will make its way into the world with its private traumas. Life under political oppression has begun to yield, in the slow bitter way it does, a rich intellectual and artistic harvest: Peer's memoir *Curfewed Night* was followed in 2011 by *The Collaborator*, a searing novel by Mirza Waheed. There are more works to come; Kashmiris will increasingly speak for themselves. One can only hope that their voices will finally penetrate our indifference and even occasionally prick our conscience.

Tariq Ali

The Story of Kashmir

Only graveyard breezes blow in the valley of Kashmir. Murder tours the region in different guises, garbed sometimes in the uniform of the Indian army or in the form of bearded men, armed and infiltrated by Pakistan, speaking the language of jihad— Allah and Fate rolled into one. The background presence of nuclear missiles offers a ghoulish comfort to both sides. Kashmir, trapped in this neither–nor predicament, suffocates. Depressed and exhausted by the decades of violence, many Kashmiris have become passive: the beauties of spring and summer pass unnoticed by listless eyes. Yet, fearful even of medium-term possibilities, Kashmiris prefer to live in the present. Oppressed by neither–nor, they are silent in public, speaking the truth in whispers. They fear that old Kabul might move to Srinagar and, in the name of a petrified religion, ban all poetry and music, outlaw the public appearance of unveiled women, close down the university and impose a clerical dictatorship. It is difficult to imagine a Talibanized Kashmir, but it was once equally diffi-cult to imagine a Talibanized Afghanistan. A complicated and unpredictable combination of circumstances does sometimes enable the enemies of light to triumph. Unless . . .

I was thinking about this on a balmy October evening in New York during the dying days of the Clinton presidency, wondering if there was an alternative to neither–nor and what, if anything, the Empire had in store for its South Asian satrapies. Provincial at the best of times, the country was immersed in its own election campaign.

Strolling down Eighth Avenue in search of sustenance, I was halted between 40th and 41st streets by a tacky, twinkling, neon-lit sign: K-A-S-H-M-I-R. An adjacent, non-twinkling arrow signalled a fast-food dive in the basement below. I decided to risk the food. Attached to the austere eating zone was an extension in the shape of a raised wooden platform. A slab on the wall proclaimed this to be Jinnah Hall, inaugurated in 1996 by Nawaz Sharif, the prime minister of Pakistan. I asked the young Kashmiri woman sitting behind the cash desk underneath the slab whether this could possibly be the same Nawaz Sharif who was sitting at the time in a Pakistani prison on charges of corruption and attempted murder. She smiled, but did not reply. Instead she turned her eyes to the 'Hall', where a meeting was in progress. The place was nearly full. About twenty or so South Asian men and a single white woman. The top table was occupied by an assortment of beards dressed in traditional baggy trousers and long shirts. I felt for one of them. Afflicted with the dreaded dhobi's itch, he was engaged in his own private jihad, scratching away at his testicles throughout the evening.

At the lectern, next to the top table, a clean-shaven white American was already in full flow. His gestures and rancid rhetoric suggested a politician, who could have belonged to either party. He turned out to be a Democratic congressman, 'a friend of the people of Kashmir'. Recently returned from a visit to the country, he had been 'deeply moved' by the suffering he had witnessed and was now convinced that 'the moral leadership of the world must take up this issue'. The beards nodded vigorously, recalling no doubt the help the 'moral leadership' had given in Kabul and Kosovo. The congressman paused; he didn't want to mislead these people. What was on offer was not a 'humanitarian war' but an informal Camp David. 'It needn't even be the United States,' he continued. 'It could be a great man. It could be Nelson Mandela . . . or Bill Clinton.'

The beards were unimpressed. One of the few beardless men in the audience rose to his feet and addressed the congressman: 'Please answer honestly to our worries,' he said. 'In Afghanistan we helped you defeat the Red Army. You needed us then and we were very much loyal to you. Now you have abandoned us for India. Mr Clinton supports India, not human rights in Kashmir. Is this a good way to treat very old friends?'

The congressman made sympathetic noises, even promising to tick Clinton off for not being 'more vigorous on human rights in Kashmir'. He needn't have bothered. A beard rose to ask why the US government had betrayed them. The repetition irritated the congressman. He took the offensive, complaining about this being an all-male meeting. Why were these men's wives and daughters not present? The bearded faces remained impassive. Feeling the need for some fresh air, I decided to leave. As I went up the stairs the congressman changed tack once again, speaking now of the wondrous beauty of the valley he had recently visited.

Damn the beauty, I thought, stop the killings. Were the congressman or attendant beards aware of Kashmir's turbulent past, Islamic and pre-Islamic? Did they know that the Mughal kings had never regarded religion as a cornerstone of empire-building? Were they aware of the strong women who had resisted rulers in the past, or why Kashmir had been sold for a pittance by the East India Company to a corrupt local ruler? And why it had all ended so badly? Could the beards seriously imagine that the Empire would intervene and transform Srinagar into Sarajevo, occupied by Western troops while India and China watched calmly from the sidelines? Or did they believe that one day a totally bearded Pakistan would use nuclear missiles to liberate them?

'The buildings of Kashmir are all of wood,' the Mughal emperor Jehangir wrote in his memoirs in March 1622. 'They make them two, three and four-storeyed, and covering the roofs with earth, they plant bulbs of the black tulip, which blooms year after year with the arrival of spring and is exceedingly beautiful. This custom is peculiar to the people of Kashmir. This year, in the little garden of the palace and on the roof of the largest mosque, the tulips blossomed luxuriantly . . . The flowers that are seen in the territories of Kashmir are beyond all calculation.' Surveying the lakes and waterfalls, the roses, irises and jasmine, he described the valley as 'a page that the painter of destiny had drawn with the pencil of creation'.

The first Muslim invasion of Kashmir took place in the eighth century and was defeated by the Himalayas. The soldiers of the Prophet found it impossible to move beyond the mountains' southern slopes. Their victory came unexpectedly five centuries later, as a result of a palace coup carried out by Rinchana, the Buddhist chief from neighbouring Ladakh, who had sought refuge in Kashmir and embraced Islam under the guidance of a Sufi with the pleasing name of Bulbul ('Nightingale') Shah. Rinchana's conversion would have been neither here nor there had it not been for the Turkish mercenaries who made up the ruler's elite guard and who were only too pleased to switch their allegiance to a co-religionist. But they swore to obey only the new ruler, not his descendants, so when Rinchana died, the leader of the mercenaries, Shah Mir, took control and founded the first Muslim dynasty to rule Kashmir. It lasted for seven hundred years.

The population, however, was not easily swayed, and despite a policy of forced conversion, it wasn't until the end of the reign of Zain-al-Abidin in the late fifteenth century that a majority of Kashmiris embraced Islam. In fact, Zain-al-Abidin, an inspired ruler, ended the forced conversion of Hindus and decreed that those who had been converted in this fashion be allowed to return to their own faith. He even provided Hindus with subsidies to enable them to rebuild the temples his father had destroyed. The different ethnic and religious groups still weren't allowed to intermarry, but they learned to live side by side amicably enough. Zain-al-Abidin organized visits to Iran and Central Asia so that his subjects could learn bookbinding and woodcarving and how to make carpets and shawls, thereby laying the foundations for the shawl making for which Kashmir is famous. By the end of his reign a large majority of the population had converted voluntarily to Islam; the ratio of Muslims to non-Muslims—85 per cent to 15 per cent—has remained fairly constant ever since.

The dynasty went into a decline after Zain-al-Abidin's death. Disputes over the succession, unfit rulers, and endless intrigues among the nobility paved the way for new invasions. In the end, the Mughal conquest in the late sixteenth century probably came as a relief to most people. The landlords were replaced by Mughal civil servants who administered the country rather more efficiently, reorganizing its trade, its shawl making and its agriculture. On the other hand, deprived of local patronage, Kashmir's poets, painters and scribes left the valley in search of employment at the Mughal courts in Delhi and Lahore, taking the country's cultural life with them.

What made the disappearance of Kashmiri culture particularly harsh was the fact that the conquest itself had coincided with a sudden flowering of the Kashmiri court. Zoonie, the wife of Sultan Yusuf Shah, was a peasant from the village of Tsandahar who had been taken up by a Sufi mystic enchanted with her voice. Under his guidance she learned Persian and began to write her own songs. One day, passing with his entourage and hearing her voice in the fields, Yusuf Shah, too, was captivated. He took her to court and prevailed on her to marry him. And that is how Zoonie entered the palace as queen and took the name of Habba Khatun ('Loved Woman'). She wrote:

> I thought I was indulging in play, and lost myself.
> O for the day that is dying!
> At home I was secluded, unknown,
> When I left home, my fame spread far and wide,
> The pious laid all their merit at my feet.
> O for the day that is dying!
> My beauty was like a warehouse filled with rare merchandise,
> Which drew men from all the four quarters;
> Now my richness is gone, I have no worth:
> O for the day that is dying!
> My father's people were of high standing,
> I became known as Habba Khatun:
> O for the day that is dying.

Habba Khatun gave the Kashmiri language a literary form and encouraged a synthesis of Persian and Indian musical styles. She gave women the freedom to decorate themselves as they wished and revived the old Circassian tradition of tattooing the face and hands with special dyes and powders. The clerics were furious. They saw in her the work of Iblis, or Satan, in league with the blaspheming, licentious Sufis. While Yusuf Shah remained on the throne, however, Habba Khatun was untouchable. She mocked the pretensions of the clergy, defended the mystic strain within Islam and compared herself to a flower that flourishes in fertile soil and cannot be uprooted.

Habba Khatun was queen when, in 1583, the Mughal emperor Akbar dispatched his favourite general to annex the kingdom of Kashmir. There was no fighting: Yusuf Shah rode out to the Mughal camp and capitulated without a struggle, demanding only the right to retain the throne and strike coins in his image. Instead, he was arrested and sent into exile. The Kashmiri nobles, angered by Yusuf Shah's betrayal, placed his son Yakub Shah on the throne, but Yakub was a weak and intemperate young man who set the Sunni and Shia clerics at one another's throats, and before long Akbar sent a large expeditionary force, which took Kashmir in the summer of 1588. In the autumn the emperor came to see the valley's famous colours for himself.

Habba Khatun's situation changed dramatically after Akbar had her husband exiled. Unlike Sughanda and Dida, two powerful tenth-century queens who had ascended the throne as regents, Habba Khatun was driven out of the palace. At first she found refuge with the Sufis, but after a time she began to move from village to village, giving voice in her songs to the melancholy of a suppressed people. There is no record of when or where she died – a grave thought to be hers was discovered in the middle of the last century – but women mourning the disappearance of young men killed by the Indian army or 'volunteered' to fight in the jihad still sing her verses:

Who told him where I lived?
Why has he left me in such anguish?
I, hapless one, am filled with longing for him.
He glanced at me through my window,
He who is as lovely as my ear-rings;
He has made my heart restless:
I, hapless one, am filled with longing for him.
He glanced at me through the crevice in my roof,
Sang like a bird that I might look at him,
Then, soft-footed, vanished from my sight:
I, hapless one, am filled with longing for him.
He glanced at me while I was drawing water,
I withered like a red rose,
My soul and body were ablaze with love:
I, hapless one, am filled with longing for him.
He glanced at me in the waning moonlight of early dawn,
Stalked me like one obsessed.
Why did he stoop so low?
I, hapless one, am filled with longing for him!

Habba Khatun exemplified a gentle version of Islam, diluted with pre-Islamic practices and heavily influenced by Sufi mysticism. This tradition is still strong in the countryside and helps to explain Kashmiri indifference to the more militant forms of religion.

The Mughal emperors were drawn to their new domain. Akbar's son Jehangir lost his fear of death there, since only Paradise could transcend the beauties of Kashmir. While his wife and brother-in-law kept their eye on the administration of the empire, he reflected on his luck at having escaped the plains of the Punjab and spent his time smoking opium, sampling the juice of the Kashmir grape, and planning gardens around natural springs so that the reflection of the rising and setting sun could be seen in the water that cascaded down specially constructed channels. 'If on earth there be a paradise of bliss, it is this, it is this, it is this,' he wrote, citing a well-known Persian couplet.

By the eighteenth century, the Mughal empire had begun its own slow decline, and the Kashmiri nobles invited Ahmed Shah Durrani, the brutal ruler of Afghanistan, to liberate their country. Durrani obliged in 1752, doubling taxes and persecuting the embattled Shia minority with a fanatical vigour that shocked the nobles. Fifty years of Afghan rule were punctuated by regular clashes between Sunni and Shia Muslims.

Worse lay ahead, however. In 1819, the soldiers of Ranjit Singh, the charismatic leader of the Sikhs, already triumphant in northern India, took Srinagar. There was no resistance worth the name. Kashmiri historians regard the twenty-seven years of Sikh rule that followed as the worst calamity ever to befall their country. The principal mosque in Srinagar was closed, others were made the property of the state, cow-slaughter was prohibited, and once again the tax burden became insufferable – unlike the Mughals, Ranjit Singh taxed the poor. Mass impoverishment led to mass emigration. Kashmiris fled to the cities of the Punjab: Amritsar, Lahore and Rawalpindi became the new centres of Kashmiri life and culture. (One of the many positive effects of this influx was that Kashmiri cooks greatly improved the local food.)

Sikh rule didn't last long: new conquerors were on the way. What was possibly the most remarkable enterprise in the history of mercantile capitalism had launched itself on the Indian subcontinent. Granted semi-sovereign powers – that is, the right to maintain armies – by the British and Dutch states, the East India Company expanded rapidly from its Calcutta base and, after the battle of Plassey in 1757, took the whole of Bengal. Within a few years the Mughal emperor at the fort in Delhi had become a pensioner of the Company, whose forces continued to move west, determined now to take the Punjab from the Sikhs. The first Anglo-Sikh war, in 1846, resulted in a victory for the Company, which acquired Kashmir as part of the Treaty of Amritsar, but, aware of the chaos there, hurriedly sold it for seventy-five lakh rupees (ten lakhs = one million) to the Dogra ruler of neighbouring Jammu, who pushed through yet more taxes. When, after the 1857 uprising, the East India Company was replaced by direct rule from London, real power in Kashmir and other princely states devolved on a British Resident, usually a fresh face from Haileybury College serving an apprenticeship in the backwaters of the empire.

Kashmir suffered badly under its Dogra rulers. The corvée was reintroduced after the collapse of the Mughal state, and the peasants were reduced to the condition of serfs. A story, unconfirmable, told by Kashmiri intellectuals in the 1920s to highlight the plight of the peasants revolved round the maharaja's purchase of a Cadillac. When His Highness drove the car to Pehalgam, admiring peasants surrounded it and strewed fresh grass in front of it. The maharaja acknowledged their presence by letting them touch the car. A few peasants began to cry. 'Why are you crying?' asked their ruler. 'We arc upset', one of them replied, 'because your new animal refuses to eat grass.'

When it finally reached the valley, the twentieth century brought new values: freedom from foreign rule, passive resistance, the right to form trade unions, even socialism. Young Kashmiris educated in Lahore and Delhi returned home determined to wrench their country from the stranglehold of the

Dogra maharaja and his colonial patrons. When the Muslim poet and philosopher Iqbal, himself of Kashmiri origin, visited Srinagar in 1921, he left behind a subversive couplet which spread around the country:

> In the bitter chill of winter shivers his naked body
> Whose skill wraps the rich in royal shawls.

Kashmiri workers went on strike for the first time in the spring of 1924. Five thousand workers in the state-owned silk factory demanded a pay rise and the dismissal of a clerk who'd been running a protection racket. The management agreed to a small increase, but arrested the leaders of the protest. The workers then came out on strike. With the backing of the British Resident, the opium-sodden Maharaja Pratap Singh sent in troops. Workers on the picket line were badly beaten, suspected ringleaders were sacked on the spot and the principal organizer of the action was imprisoned, then tortured to death.

Some months later, a group of ultra-conservative Muslim notables in Srinagar sent a memorandum to the British viceroy, Lord Reading, protesting the brutality and repression:

> Military was sent for and most inhuman treatment was meted out to the poor, helpless, unarmed, peace-loving labourers who were assaulted with spears, lances and other implements of warfare . . . The Mussulmans of Kashmir are in a miserable plight today. Their education is woefully neglected. Though forming 96 per cent of the population, the percentage of literacy amongst them is only 0.8 per cent . . . So far we have patiently borne the state's indifference towards our grievances and our

claims and its high-handedness towards our rights, but patience
has its limit and resignation its end.

The viceroy forwarded the petition to the maharaja, who
was enraged. He wanted the 'sedition-mongers' shot, but the
Resident wouldn't have it. As a sop he ordered the immediate
deportation of the organizer of the petition, Saaduddin Shawl.
Nothing changed even when, a few years later, the maharaja died
and was replaced by his nephew, Hari Singh. Albion Bannerji,
the new British-approved chief minister of Kashmir, found the
situation intolerable. Frustrated by his inability to achieve even
trivial reforms, he resigned. 'The large Muslim population', he
said, 'is absolutely illiterate, labouring under poverty and very
low economic conditions of living in the villages and practically
governed like dumb driven cattle.'

In April 1931, the police entered the mosque in Jammu and
stopped the Friday *khutba* which follows the prayers. The
police chief claimed that references in the Quran to Moses and
Pharaoh quoted by the preacher were tantamount to sedition. It
was an exceptionally stupid thing to do and, inevitably, it triggered a new wave of protests. In June, the largest political rally
ever seen in Srinagar elected eleven representatives by popular acclamation to lead the struggle against native and colonial
repression. Among them was Sheikh Abdullah, the son of a
shawl trader, who would dominate the life of Kashmir for the
next half-century.

One of the less well-known speakers at the rally, Abdul
Qadir, a butler who worked for a European household, was
arrested for having described the Dogra rulers as 'a dynasty of
blood-suckers' who had 'drained the energies and resources of
all our people'. On the first day of Qadir's trial, thousands of

demonstrators gathered outside the prison and demanded the right to attend the proceedings. The police opened fire, killing twenty-one of them. Sheikh Abdullah and other political leaders were arrested the following day. This was the founding moment of Kashmiri nationalism.

At the same time, a parturition was taking place on the French Riviera. Tara Devi, the fourth wife of the dissolute and infertile Maharaja Hari Singh – he had shunted aside the first three for failing to produce any children – gave birth to a boy, Karan Singh. In the Srinagar bazaar every second person claimed to have fathered the heir-apparent. Five days of lavish entertainment and feasting marked the infant heir's arrival in Srinagar. A few weeks later, public agitation broke out, punctuated by lampoons concerning the maharaja's lack of sexual prowess, among other things. The authorities sanctioned the use of public flogging, but it was too late. Kashmir could no longer be quarantined from a subcontinent eager for independence.

The viceroy instructed the maharaja to release the imprisoned nationalist leaders, who were carried through the streets of Srinagar on the shoulders of triumphant crowds. The infant Karan Singh had been produced in vain; he would never inherit his father's dominion. Many years later he wrote of his father:

> He was a bad loser. Any small setback in shooting or fishing, polo or racing, would throw him in a dark mood which lasted for days. And this would inevitably lead to what became known as a *muqaddama*, a long inquiry into the alleged inefficiency or misbehaviour of some hapless young member of staff or a servant . . . Here was authority without generosity; power without compassion.

On their release from jail, Sheikh Abdullah and his colleagues set about establishing a political organization capable of uniting Muslims and non-Muslims. The All–Jammu and Kashmir Muslim Conference was founded in Srinagar in October 1932, and Abdullah was elected its president. Non-Muslims in Kashmir were mainly Hindus, dominated by the Pandits, upper-caste Brahmins who looked down on Muslims, Sikhs and low-caste Hindus alike, but looked up to their colonial masters, as they had to the Mughals. The British, characteristically, used the Pandits to run the administration, making it easy for Muslims to see the two enemies as one. Abdullah, though a Quranic scholar, was resolutely secular in his politics. The Hindus might be a tiny minority of the population, but he knew it would be fatal for Kashmiri interests if the Brahmins were ignored or persecuted. The confessional Muslims led by Mirwaiz Yusuf Shah broke away – the split was inevitable – accusing Abdullah of being soft on Hindus as well as on those Muslims regarded by the orthodox as heretics. From the All-India Kashmir Committee in Lahore came an angry poster addressed by the poet Iqbal to the 'dumb Muslims of Kashmir'.

No longer constrained by the orthodox faction in his own ranks, Sheikh Abdullah drew closer to the social-revolutionary nationalism advocated by Nehru. He wasn't the only Muslim leader to do so: Khan Abdul Ghaffar Khan in the Northwest Frontier Province, Mian Iftikharuddin in the Punjab, and Maulana Azad in the United Provinces all decided to work with the Indian National Congress, but this was not enough to tempt the majority of educated urban Muslims away from the Muslim League.

The Muslims had arrived in India as conquerors. They saw their religion as infinitely superior to that of the idol-worshipping

Hindus and Buddhists. The bulk of Indian Muslims were none the less converts: some forced and others voluntary, seeking escape, in Kashmir and Bengal especially, from the rigours of the caste system. Thus, despite itself, Islam in India – as in coastal Africa, China and the Indonesian archipelago – was affected by local religious practices. Muslim saints were worshipped like Hindu gods. Holy men and ascetics were incorporated into Indian Islam. The Prophet Muhammad came to be regarded as a divinity. Buddhism had been especially strong in Kashmir, and the Buddhist worship of relics, too, was transferred to Islam, so that Kashmir is the home today of one of the holiest Muslim relics: a strand of hair supposedly belonging to Muhammad. The Quran expressly disavows necromancy, magic and omens, and yet these superstitions remain a strong part of subcontinental Islam. Many Muslim political leaders still have favourite astrologers and soothsayers.

Muslim nationalism in India was the product of defeat. Until the collapse of the Mughal empire at the hands of the British, Muslims had dominated the ruling class for more than five hundred years. With the disappearance of the Mughal court in Delhi and the culture it supported, they were now merely a large religious minority considered by Hindus as lower than the lowest Hindu caste. There was an abrupt retreat from the Persian–Hindu cultural synthesis they had created, orphaning the scribes, poets, traders and artisans who had flourished around the old Muslim courts. The poet Akbar Allahabadi (1846–1921) became the voice of India's dispossessed Muslims, speaking for a community in decline:

> The Englishman is happy, he owns the aeroplane,
> The Hindu's gratified, he controls all the trade,

'Tis we who are empty drums, subsisting on God's grace,
 • A pile of biscuit crumbs and frothy lemonade.

The angry and embittered leaders of the Muslim community
asked believers to wage a jihad against the infidel and to boycott
everything he represented. The chief result was a near-terminal
decline in Muslim education and intellectual life. In the 1870s,
Syed Ahmad Khan, pleading for compromise, warned Muslims
that their self-imposed isolation would have terrible economic
consequences. In 1875, in the hope of encouraging them to abandon the religious schools, where they were taught the Quoran by
rote in a language they couldn't understand, he established the
Muslim Anglo-Oriental College in Aligarh, which became the
pre-eminent Muslim university in the country. Men and women
from all over northern India were sent there to be educated in
English as well as Urdu.

It was here, at the end of the 1920s, that Sheikh Abdullah
had enrolled as a student. The college authorities encouraged
Muslims to stay away from politics, but by the time Sheikh
Abdullah arrived in Aligarh, students were divided into liberal
and conservative camps and it was difficult to avoid debates
on religion, nationalism and communism. Even the most dull-
witted among them – usually those from feudal families – got
involved. Most of the nationalist Muslims at Aligarh University
aligned themselves with the Indian National Congress rather
than the Muslim League, which had been set up by the Aga
Khan on the viceroy's behalf.

To demonstrate his commitment to secular politics,
Sheikh Abdullah invited Nehru to Kashmir. Nehru, whose
forebears were Kashmiri Pandits, brought with him Abdul
Ghaffar Khan, the Frontier Gandhi. The three leaders spoke

at consciousness-raising meetings and addressed groups of workers, intellectuals, peasants and women. What the visitors enjoyed most, however, was loitering in the old Mughal gardens. Like everyone else, Nehru had a go at describing the valley:

> Like some supremely beautiful woman, whose beauty is almost impersonal and above human desire, such was Kashmir in all its feminine beauty of river and valley and lake and graceful trees. And then another aspect of this magic beauty would come into view, a masculine one, of hard mountains and precipices, and snow-capped peaks and glaciers, and cruel and fierce torrents rushing to the valleys below. It had a hundred faces and innumerable aspects, ever-changing, sometimes smiling, sometimes sad and full of sorrow . . . I watched this spectacle and sometimes the sheer loveliness of it was overpowering and I felt faint . . . It seemed to me dreamlike and unreal, like the hopes and desires that fill us and so seldom find fulfilment. It was like the face of the beloved that one sees in a dream and that fades away on wakening.

Sheikh Abdullah promised liberation from Dogra rule and pledged land reform; Nehru preached the virtues of unremitting struggle against the empire and insisted that social reform could come only after the departure of the British; Ghaffar Khan spoke of the need for mass struggle and urged Kashmiris to throw fear to the wind: 'You who live in the valleys must learn to scale the highest peaks.'

Nehru knew that the main reason they had been showered with affection was that Abdullah had been with them. There was now a strong political bond between the two men, unlike as they were. Abdullah was a Muslim from a humble background whose outlook remained provincial and whose political views arose from a hatred of suffering and of the social injustice he perceived to be its cause. Nehru, a product of Harrow and Cambridge, was a lofty figure, conscious of his own intellectual superiority, rarely afflicted by fear or envy, and always intolerant of fools. He was a left-wing internationalist and a staunch anti-fascist. Yet the ties established between the pair proved vital for Kashmir when separatism took over the subcontinent in 1947.

In a hangover from Mughal days, and to make up for their lack of real power, the Muslims of India had developed an irritating habit of inflating their leaders with fancy titles. In this scheme, Sheikh Abdullah became Sher-i-Kashmir, the Lion of Kashmir, and his wife, Akbar Jehan, Madri-i-Meharban, the Kind Mother. The Lion depended on the Kind Mother to impress famous visitors, to receive them during his frequent absences in prison, and to give him sound political advice. Akbar Jehan was the daughter of Harry Nedous, an Austro-Swiss hotelier, and Mir Jan, a Kashmiri milkmaid. The Nedous family had arrived in India at the turn of the last century and had invested its savings in the majestic Nedous Hotel in Lahore – later there were hotels in Srinagar and Poona. Harry Nedous was the businessman; his brothers, Willy and Wally, willied and wallied around; his sister, Enid, took charge of the catering, and her pâtisserie at their Lahore hotel was considered 'as good as anything in Europe'.

Harry Nedous first caught sight of Mir Jan when she came to deliver the milk at his holiday lodge in Gulmarg. He was immediately smitten, but she was suspicious. 'I might be poor,' she told him later that week, 'but I am not for sale.' Harry pleaded that he was serious, that he loved her, that he wanted to marry her. 'In that case,' she retorted wrathfully, 'you must convert to Islam. I cannot marry an unbeliever.' To her amazement he did so, and in time they had twelve children (only five of whom survived). Brought up as a devout Muslim, their daughter Akbar Jehan was a boarder at the Convent of Jesus and Mary in the hill resort of Murree. Non-Christian parents often packed their daughters off to these convents because the education was quite good and the regime strict, though there is evidence to suggest that the students spent much of their time fantasizing about Rudolph Valentino.

In 1928, when the seventeen-year-old Akbar Jehan had left school and was back in Lahore, a senior figure in British Military Intelligence checked in to the Nedous Hotel on the Upper Mall. Colonel T. E. Lawrence, complete with Valentino-style headgear, had just spent a gruelling few weeks in Afghanistan destabilizing the radical, modernizing and anti-British regime of King Amanullah. Disguised as 'Karam Shah', a visiting Arab cleric, he had organized a black propaganda campaign designed to stoke the religious fervour of the more reactionary tribes and thus provoke a civil war. His mission accomplished, he left for Lahore. Akbar Jehan must have met him at her father's hotel. A flirtation began and got out of control. Her father insisted that they get married immediately, which they did. Three months later, in January 1929, Amanullah was toppled and replaced by a pro-British ruler. On 12 January, Kipling's old newspaper in Lahore, the imperialist *Civil and Military Gazette*, published comparative profiles of Lawrence and 'Karam Shah' to reinforce the impression that they were two different people. Several weeks later, the Calcutta newspaper *Liberty* reported that 'Karam Shah' was indeed the 'British spy Lawrence' and gave a detailed account of his activities in Waziristan on the Afghan frontier. Lawrence was becoming a liability, and the authorities told him to return to Britain. 'Karam Shah' was never seen again. Nedous insisted on a divorce for his daughter, and again Lawrence obliged. Four years later, Sheikh Abdullah and Akbar Jehan were married in Srinagar. The fact of her previous marriage and divorce was never a secret: only the real name of her first husband was hidden. She now threw herself into the struggle for a new Kashmir. She raised money to build schools for poor children and encouraged adult education in a state where the bulk of the population was illiterate. She also, crucially, gave support and advice to her husband, alerting him, for example, to the dangers of succumbing to Nehru's charm and thus compromising his own standing in Kashmir.

Few politicians in the 1930s believed that the subcontinent would ever be divided along religious lines. Even the most ardent Muslim separatists were prepared to accept a federation based on the principle of regional autonomy. In the 1937 elections the Congress Party swept most of the country, including the Muslim-majority North-West Frontier Province, where Ghaffar Khan's popularity was at its peak. The Muslim-majority provinces of the Punjab and Bengal remained loyal to the raj and voted for secular parties controlled by the landed gentry. Contrary to Pakistani mythology, separatism wasn't at this stage an aim so much as a bargaining tool to ensure that Muslims received a fair share of the post-colonial spoils.

The Second World War changed everything. India was included in Britain's declaration of war against Germany, and the Congress Party was livid at His Majesty's government's failure to consult them. Nehru would probably have argued in favour of participating in the anti-fascist struggle provided the

British agreed to leave India once it was all over, and London would probably have regarded such a request as impertinent. As it was, the Congress governments of each province resigned. Gandhi, who despite his pacifism had acted as an efficient recruiting sergeant for the British during the First World War, was less sure what to do this time. A hard-line ultra-nationalist current within the Congress, led by the charismatic Bengali Subhas Chandra Bose, argued for an alliance with Britain's enemies, particularly Japan. This was unacceptable to Nehru and Gandhi. But when Singapore fell, in 1942, Gandhi, like most observers, was sure that the Japanese were about to take India by way of Bengal and argued that the Congress had to oppose the British empire, whatever the cost, in order to gain a position to strike a deal with the Japanese. The wartime coalition in London sent Stafford Cripps to woo the Congress back into line. He offered its leaders a 'blank cheque' after the war. 'What is the point of a blank cheque from a bank that is already failing?' Gandhi replied. In August 1942, the Congress leaders authorized the launch of the Quit India movement. A tidal wave of civil disobedience swept the country. The entire Congress leadership, including Gandhi and Nehru, was arrested, as were thousands of organizers and workers. The Muslim League backed the war effort and prospered. Partition was the ultimate prize.

When Nehru and Ghaffar Khan revisited Srinagar as Abdullah's guests in the summer of 1945, it was evident that divisions between the different nationalists were acute. The Lion of Kashmir had laid on a Mughal-style welcome. The guests were taken downriver on lavishly decorated *shikaras* (gondolas). Barred from gathering on the four bridges along the route, Abdullah's local Muslim opponents stood on the embankment, dressed in *phirens*, long tunics which almost touched the ground. In the summer months it was customary not to wear underclothes. As the boats approached, the male protesters, who had not been allowed to carry banners, faced the guests and lifted their *phirens* to reveal their pencils of creation, while the women turned their backs and bared their buttocks. Muslims had never protested in this way before, and have not done so since. Ghaffar Khan roared with laughter, but Nehru was not amused. Later that day Ghaffar Khan referred to the episode at a rally and told the audience how impressed he had been by the wares on display. Nehru, asked at a dinner the next day how he compared the regions he had visited most recently, replied: 'Punjabis are crude, Bengalis are hysterical, and the Kashmiris are simply vulgar.'

The confessional movement was gaining strength, however. Mohammed Ali Jinnah, the founding father of Pakistan, had left the Congress in the 1930s, partly because he was uneasy about Gandhi's use of Hindu religious imagery. He had then joined the Muslim League in a partially successful attempt to wrest it from the collaborationist landlords of the United Provinces. Jinnah had half-hoped, half-believed that Pakistan would be a smaller version of India, but one in which Muslims would dominate, with Hindus and Sikhs still living there and forming a loyal minority. Had a confederal solution been adopted this might have been possible, but once the decision to split the country had been accepted as irrevocable by the departing British, it was out of the question. Bengal and the Punjab were mixed provinces, and so they, too, would have to be divided. As they were.

Crimes were committed by all sides. Those who were reluctant to abandon their villages were driven out or massacred. Trains carrying refugee families were attacked by armed gangs and became moving coffins. There are no agreed-upon figures, but according to the lowest estimates, the slicing of the subcontinent cost nearly a million lives. No official monument marks the casualties of Partition; there is no official record of those who perished. Amrita Pritam, an eighteen-year-old Sikh, born and brought up in Lahore but now forced to become a refugee, left behind a lament in which she evoked the medieval Sufi poet and freethinker Waris Shah, whose love epic *Heer-Ranjha* was (and is) sung in almost every Punjabi village on both sides of the divide:

> I call Waris Shah today:
> 'Speak up from your grave,
> From your Book of Love unfurl
> A new and different page.
> *One* daughter of the Punjab did scream,
> You covered our walls with your laments.'
> Millions of daughters weep today
> And call out to Waris Shah:
> 'Arise you chronicler of our inner pain
> And look now at your Punjab;
> The forests are littered with corpses
> And blood flows down the Chenab.'

Kashmir is the unfinished business of Partition. The agreement to divide the subcontinent had entailed referendums and elections in the Muslim-majority segments of British India. In the North-West Frontier Province, which was 90 per cent Muslim, the Muslim League had defeated the anti-Partition forces led by Ghaffar Khan. It did so by intimidation, chicanery and selective violence. The Muslim League never won a free election there again, and Ghaffar Khan spent much of the rest of his life – he died in the 1980s – in a Pakistani prison, accused of treason. His defeat seemed to prove that secular Muslim leaders, despite their popularity, were powerless against the confessional tide. Would Sheikh Abdullah be able to preserve a united Kashmir?

In constitutional terms, Kashmir was a 'princely state', which meant that its maharaja had the legal right to choose whether to accede to India or to Pakistan. In cases where the ruler did not share the faith of a large majority of his population, it was assumed he would nevertheless go along with the wishes of the people. In Hyderabad and Junagadh – Hindu majority, Muslim royals – the rulers wobbled, but finally chose India. Jinnah began to woo the maharaja of Kashmir in the hope that he would decide in favour of Pakistan. This enraged Sheikh Abdullah. Hari Singh vacillated.

Kashmir's accession was still unresolved when midnight struck on 14 August 1947 and the Union Jack was lowered for the last time. Independence. There were now two armies in the subcontinent, each commanded by a British officer and with a very large proportion of British officers in the senior ranks. Lord Mountbatten, the governor-general of India, and Field Marshal Auchinleck, the joint commander-in-chief of both armies, made it clear to Jinnah that the use of force in Kashmir would not be tolerated. If it were attempted, Britain would withdraw every British officer from the Pakistan army. Pakistan backed down. The League's traditional toadying to the British played a part in this decision, but there were other factors: Britain exercised a great deal of economic leverage; Mountbatten's authority was resented but could not be ignored; Pakistan's civil servants hadn't yet much self-confidence. And, unknown to his people, Jinnah was dying of tuberculosis. Besides, Pakistan's first prime minister, Liaquat Ali Khan, an upper-class refugee from India, was not in any sense a rebel. He had worked too closely with the departing colonial power to want to thwart it. He had no feel for the politics of the regions that now comprised Pakistan and he didn't get on with the Muslim landlords who dominated the League in the Punjab. They wanted to run the country and would soon have him killed, but not just yet.

Meanwhile, something had to be done about Kashmir. There was unrest in the army, and even secular politicians felt that Kashmir, as a Muslim state, should form part of Pakistan. The maharaja had begun to negotiate secretly with India, and a desperate Jinnah decided to authorize a military operation in defiance of the British high command. Pakistan would advance into Kashmir and seize Srinagar. Jinnah nominated a younger colleague from the Punjab, Sardar Shaukat Hyat Khan, to take charge of the operation.

Shaukat had served as a captain during the war and had spent several months in an Italian POW camp. On his return he had resigned his commission and joined the Muslim League. He was one of its more popular leaders in the Punjab, devoted to Jinnah, extremely hostile to Liaquat, whom he regarded as an arriviste, and keen to earn the title Lion of the Punjab, which was occasionally chanted in his honour at public meetings. An effete and vainglorious figure, easily swayed by flattery, Shaukat was a chocolate-cream soldier. The unexpected death of his father, the elected prime minister of the old Punjab, had brought him to prominence. He was not one of those people who rise above their own shortcomings in a crisis. I knew him well: he was my uncle. To his credit, he argued against the use of irregulars and wanted the operation to be restricted to retired or serving military personnel. He was overruled by the prime

minister, who insisted that his loud-mouthed protégé, Khurshid
Anwar, take part in the operation. Anwar, against all military
advice, enlisted Pashtun tribesmen in the cause of jihad. Two
extremely able brigadiers, Akbar Khan and Sher Khan from the
6/13th Frontier Force Regiment ('Piffers' to old India hands),
were selected to lead the assault.

The invasion was fixed for 9 September 1947, but it had to be
delayed for two weeks: Khurshid Anwar had chosen the same
day to get married and wanted to go on a brief honeymoon.
In the meantime, thanks to Anwar's lack of discretion, a senior
Pakistani officer, Brigadier Iftikhar, heard what was going on
and passed the news to General Messervy, the commander-
in-chief of the Pakistan army. He immediately informed
Auchinleck, who passed the information to Mountbatten, who
passed it to the new Indian government. Using the planned
invasion as a pretext, the Congress sent Nehru's deputy, Sardar
Patel, to pressure the maharaja into acceding to India, while
Mountbatten ordered Indian army units to prepare for an emergency airlift to Srinagar.

Back in Rawalpindi, Anwar had returned from his honeymoon, and the invasion began. The key objective was to take
Srinagar, occupy the airport and secure it against the Indians.
Within a week the maharaja's army had collapsed. Hari Singh
fled to his palace in Jammu. The 11th Sikh Regiment of the
Indian army had by now reached Srinagar, but was desper-
ately waiting for reinforcements and didn't enter the town. The
Pashtun tribesmen under Khurshid Anwar's command halted
after reaching Baramulla, only an hour's bus ride from Srinagar,
and refused to go any further. Here they embarked on a three-
day binge, looting houses, assaulting Muslims and Hindus alike,
raping men and women and stealing money from the Kashmir

treasury. The local cinema was transformed into a rape centre; a group of Pashtuns invaded St Joseph's Convent, where they raped and killed four nuns, including the mother superior, and shot dead a European couple sheltering there. News of the atrocities spread, turning large numbers of Kashmiris against their would-be liberators. When they finally reached Srinagar, the Pashtuns were so intent on pillaging the shops and bazaars that they overlooked the airport, already occupied by the Sikhs.

The maharaja meanwhile signed the accession papers in favour of India and demanded help to repel the invasion. India airlifted troops and began to drive the Pakistanis back. Sporadic fighting continued until India appealed to the UN Security Council, which organized a cease-fire and a Line of Control (LOC) demarcating Indian and Pakistan-held territory. Kashmir, too, was now partitioned. The leaders of the Kashmir Muslim Conference shifted to Muzaffarabad in Pakistan-occupied Kashmir, leaving Sheikh Abdullah in control of the valley itself.

If Abdullah, too, had favoured Pakistan, there wouldn't have been much that the Indian troops could have done about it. But he regarded the Muslim League as a reactionary organization and rightly feared that if Kashmir became part of Pakistan, the Punjabi landlords who dominated the Muslim League would stand in the way of any social or political reforms. He decided to back the Indian military presence, provided the Kashmiris were allowed to determine their own future. At a mass rally in Srinagar, Nehru, with Abdullah at his side, publicly promised as much. In November 1947, Abdullah was appointed prime minister of an emergency administration. When the maharaja expressed nervousness about this, Nehru wrote to him, insisting that there was no alternative:

The only person who can deliver the goods in Kashmir is
Abdullah. I have a high opinion of his integrity and his general
balance of mind. He may make any number of mistakes in minor
matters, but I think he is likely to be right in regard to major
decisions. No satisfactory way out can be found in Kashmir
except through him.

In 1944 the National Conference had approved a constitution
for an independent Kashmir, which began:

> We the people of Jammu and Kashmir, Ladakh and the Frontier
> regions, including Poonch and Chenani districts, commonly
> known as Jammu and Kashmir State, in order to perfect our
> union in the fullest equality and self-determination, to raise
> ourselves and our children forever from the abyss of oppres-
> sion and poverty, degradation and superstition, from medieval
> darkness and ignorance, into the sunlit valleys of plenty, ruled
> by freedom, science and honest toil, in worthy participation of
> the historic resurgence of the peoples of the East, and the work-
> ing masses of the world, and in determination to make this our
> country a dazzling gem on the snowy bosom of Asia, do propose
> and propound the following constitution of our state . . .

But the 1947–8 war had made independence impossible,
and Article 370 of the Indian Constitution recognized only
Kashmir's 'special status'. True, the maharaja was replaced by
his son, Karan Singh, who became the nonhereditary head of
state, but it was a disappointed Abdullah who now sat down to
play chess with the politicians from Delhi. He knew that most
of them, apart from Gandhi and Nehru, would like to eat him
alive. For the moment, though, they needed him. Since the

split with the confessional element in the Jammu and Kashmir Conference, Abdullah had moved to the left. As the elected chief minister of Kashmir he pushed through a set of major reforms, the most important of which was the 'land to the tiller' legislation, which destroyed the power of the landlords, most of whom were Muslims. They were allowed to keep a maximum of twenty acres, provided they worked on the land themselves; meanwhile, 188,775 acres were transferred to 153,399 peasants, and the government organized collective farming on ninety thousand more. A law was passed prohibiting the sale of land to non-Kashmiris, thus preserving the basic topography of the region. Dozens of new schools and four hospitals were built, and a university was founded in Srinagar that has perhaps the most beautiful location of any campus in the world.

In the United States these reforms were regarded as communist-inspired, a viewpoint used to build support for America's new ally, Pakistan. A classic example of US propaganda of the time is *Danger in Kashmir*, written by Josef Korbel. Korbel had been a Czech UN representative in Kashmir before he defected to Washington. His book was published by Princeton in 1954, and in the second, 1966 edition, he acknowledged the 'substantial help' of several scholars, including Mrs Madeleine Albright of the Russian Institute at Columbia University – his daughter.

In 1948 the National Conference had backed 'provisional accession' to India, on condition that Kashmir would be accepted as an autonomous republic with only defence, foreign affairs and communications conceded to the centre. A small but influential minority, made up of the Dogra nobility and the Kashmiri Pandits, both fearful of losing their privileges, began to campaign against Kashmir's special status. In India proper, they were backed by the ultra-rightist Jan Sangh (which in

its current reincarnation as the Bharatiya Janata Party, or
BJP, heads the coalition government in New Delhi). The Jan
Sangh provided funds and volunteers for agitation against the
Kashmir government. Abdullah, who had gone out of his way
to integrate non-Muslims into every level of the administration, was enraged. His position hardened. At a public meeting
in the enemy stronghold of Jammu, on 10 April 1952, he made
it clear that he was not willing to surrender Kashmir's partial
sovereignty:

> Many Kashmiris are apprehensive as to what will happen to
> them and their position if, for instance, something happens to
> Pandit Nehru. We do not know. As realists, we Kashmiris have
> to provide for all eventualities . . . If there is a resurgence of
> communalism in India, how are we to convince the Muslims
> of Kashmir that India does not intend to swallow up Kashmir?

Abdullah was mistaken only in his belief that Nehru would
protect them. When the Indian prime minister visited Srinagar
in May 1953, he spent a week trying to cajole his friend into
accepting a permanent settlement on Delhi's terms: if a secular
democracy was to be preserved in India, Kashmir had to be part
of it. Nehru pleaded. Abdullah wasn't convinced: Muslims were
a large minority in India even if Kashmiris weren't included.
He felt that Nehru shouldn't be putting pressure on him but
on politicians inside the Congress who were susceptible to the
chauvinistic demands of the Jan Sangh.

Three months later, Nehru gave in to the chauvinists and
authorized what was effectively a coup in Kashmir. Sheikh
Abdullah was dismissed by Karan Singh, and one of his lieu-
tenants, Bakhshi Ghulam Mohammed, was sworn in as chief

minister. Abdullah was accused of being in contact with Pakistani intelligence and arrested. Kashmir erupted. A general strike began which was to last for twenty days. There were several thousand arrests, and Indian troops repeatedly opened fire on demonstrators. The National Conference claimed that more than a thousand people were killed; official statistics record sixty deaths. An underground war council, organized by Akbar Jehan, orchestrated demonstrations by women in Srinagar, Baramulla and Sopore.

The unrest subsided after a month, but now Kashmiris were even more suspicious of India. The situation was no happier in Pakistani-controlled Kashmir, which had the additional disadvantage of being made up of the least attractive part of the old state, a barren moonscape. Appalling living conditions gave rise to large-scale economic migration. Today, more Kashmiris live in the English cities of Birmingham and Bradford than in Mirpur or Muzaffarabad. An Islamist Kashmiri sits in the House of Lords as a New Labour peer; another Kashmiri stood as a Tory candidate in the 2001 British general elections.

Sheikh Abdullah, detained for four years without trial, was released without warning one cold morning in January 1958. Declining the offer of government transport, he hired a taxi and was driven to Srinagar. Within days he was drawing huge crowds at meetings all over the country, which he used to remind Nehru of the promise he had made in 1947. 'Why did you go back on your word, Panditji?' Abdullah would ask, and the crowds would echo the question. By spring, he had been arrested again. This time the Indian government, using British colonial legislation, began to prepare a conspiracy case against him, his wife and several other nationalist leaders. Nehru vetoed Akbar Jehan's inclusion: her popularity made it inadvisable.

The conspiracy trial began in 1959 and lasted more than a year. In 1962 the special magistrate transferred the case to a higher court with the recommendation that the accused be tried under sections of the Indian penal code for which the punishment was either death or life imprisonment.

In December 1963, with the higher court still considering the conspiracy charges, the single hair from the Prophet's head was stolen from the Hazrat Bal shrine in Srinagar. Its theft created uproar: an action committee was set up and the country was paralysed by a general strike and mass demonstrations. A distraught Nehru ordered that the strand of hair be found – and it was, within a week. But was it the real thing? The action committee called on religious leaders to inspect it. Faqir Mirak Shah, regarded as 'the holiest of the holy men', announced that it was genuine. The crisis abated. Nehru concluded that a lasting solution had to be found to the problem of Kashmir. He had the conspiracy case against Abdullah dropped, and the Lion of Kashmir was released. His second stay in prison had lasted six years. A million people lined the streets to mark his return; Nehru spoke of the necessity of ending hostilities between India and Pakistan.

Kashmir troubled Nehru's conscience. He met Abdullah in Delhi and told him that he wanted the problem of Kashmir resolved in his lifetime. He suggested that Abdullah visit Pakistan and sound out its leader, General Ayub Khan. If Pakistan was ready to accept a solution proposed by Abdullah, then Nehru would too. For a start, India was prepared to allow free movement of goods and people across the cease-fire line. Abdullah flew to Pakistan in an optimistic mood. After a series of conversations with Ayub Khan he felt progress was being made. On 27 May 1964 he reached Muzaffarabad, the capital of Pakistani-controlled Kashmir, and was cheered by a large crowd. He was addressing a press conference when a colleague rushed in to inform him that All India Radio had just announced Nehru's death. Sheikh Abdullah broke down and wept. He cancelled all his engagements and, accompanied by Pakistan's foreign minister, Zulfiqar Ali Bhutto, flew back to Delhi to attend his old friend's funeral.

Fearing that there would be no peaceful solution without Nehru, Abdullah travelled around the world, trying to get international support, and was received in several capitals with the honours accorded a visiting head of state. His meeting with the Chinese prime minister, Zhou Enlai ('Chew and Lie' in the ultra-patriotic sections of the Indian press), created a furore in India. And so, on his return, Abdullah was imprisoned again. This time he and his wife were sent to prisons far away from Kashmir. The response was the usual: strikes, demonstrations, arrests and a few deaths.

Encouraged by this, the military regime in Pakistan dispatched several platoons of irregulars in September 1965, hoping to spark off an uprising. As usual, they had misjudged the situation. The unrest was not an expression of pro-Pakistan sentiment. The Pakistan army crossed the Line of Control, aiming to cut Kashmir off from the rest of India. The military high command was confident. On the eve of the invasion, the self-appointed field marshal Ayub Khan had boasted that they might even be able to take Amritsar – the Indian town closest to Lahore – as a bargaining chip. A senior officer present (another of my uncles) muttered loudly: 'Give him a few more whiskies and we'll take Delhi as well.' The Indian army, caught by surprise, suffered serious reverses. They responded dramatically by crossing the Pakistan border near Lahore. Had the war continued, the city would have fallen, but Ayub Khan appealed to Washington for support. Washington asked Moscow to bring pressure on India, and a peace agreement was signed in Tashkent under the watchful eye of Alexei Kosygin.

The war had been Bhutto's idea. Ayub Khan, publicly humiliated at home and abroad, sacked his foreign minister. Bhutto had always been the most awkward member of the government and, embarrassed at having to serve under a general, he had ratcheted up his nationalist rhetoric. Government ministers, fearing trouble, tended to avoid the universities, but a few years before this, in 1962, Bhutto had decided to address a student meeting on Kashmir at the Punjab University in Lahore, a meeting at which I was present. He spoke eloquently enough, but we were more concerned with domestic politics. We began to talk to each other. He was offended. He stopped in mid-flow and glared at us aggressively. 'What the hell do you want? I'll answer your questions.' I raised my hand. 'We're all in favour of a democratic referendum in Kashmir,' I began, 'but we would like one in Pakistan as well. Why should anybody take you seriously on democracy in Kashmir when it doesn't exist here?'

He glared at me angrily but wouldn't be drawn, pointing out that he had only agreed to speak on Kashmir. At this point the meeting erupted, with everyone demanding a reply and chanting slogans. At one point Bhutto took off his jacket and challenged a heckler to a boxing match outside. This was greeted with jeers, and the meeting came to an abrupt halt. That night Bhutto cursed us roundly as he hurled one drained whisky glass after another against the wall, an affectation he had picked up during an official trip to Moscow. Many months later he told me that the encounter had made him realize how powerful the students were.

A week after Bhutto's dismissal, in spring 1966 – by which time I was a student in the UK – I received a phone call from J. A. Rahim, Pakistan's ambassador to France. He needed to see me in Paris the next day. He would pay my return ticket and offered the bribe of a 'sensational lunch'.

An embassy chauffeur picked me up at Orly and drove me to the restaurant. His Excellency, a cultured Bengali in his late fifties, greeted me with a conspiratorial warmth, which was surprising since we had never met. Halfway through the hors d'oeuvres he lowered his voice and asked, 'Don't you think the time has come to get rid of the Field Marshal?' Concealing my surprise, not to mention fear, I asked him to elaborate. He raised his hand above the table, pointed two fingers at me and pulled an imaginary trigger. He wanted me to help organize Ayub Khan's assassination. My instinctive reaction was to forget the main course and leave. How could this be anything other than a set-up? Rahim ordered another bottle of Château Latour, courtesy of the Pakistan government. I pointed out the danger of removing an individual military leader while leaving the institution intact. In any case, I added, it would be difficult for me to organize the assassination from Oxford. He glared at me. 'Drastic action is needed,' he said, 'and you're just trying to avoid the issue. The army is enfeebled after this wretched war. Everyone is fed up. Remove him and anything is possible. I'm surprised at you. I don't expect you to do it yourself. One of your uncles is always boasting about the hereditary assassins in your villages who've acted for your family in the past.'

I tried to talk about Kashmir, but Rahim wasn't interested. 'Kashmir', he said, 'is irrelevant. It's the dictatorship we're after.' A week later, Rahim resigned his ambassadorship. A few months after that, he turned up in London with Bhutto and summoned me to the Dorchester. I had heard that Bhutto was depressed, but there was no trace of it that day. Conscious of the shortness of life, he was the sort of man who was determined that it should flash by with brilliance, romance and verve. He could also be silly, arrogant, childish and vindictive – defects that cost him his life.

At one point, when Rahim was out of the room, I began to describe our lunch in Paris, but Bhutto already knew about it. He laughed and insisted that Rahim had just been testing me. Then he whispered, 'When you met Rahim in Paris, did he introduce you to his new mistress?' I shook my head regretfully. 'I'm told she's very pretty and very young. He's hiding her from me. I was hoping you might have . . .' Rahim came back with a bulky typescript. It was the manifesto of the Pakistan People's Party, which he had drafted on Bhutto's instructions.

'Go into the next room, read it carefully and tell me what you think,' Bhutto ordered. 'I want you to become a founding member.' I was halfway through it when the author walked in with an apologetic smile. 'Bhutto wants to be alone. He's booked a call to Geneva. Did you know he's got a Japanese mistress there? Have you met her?' I shook my head. 'He's hiding her from me,' Rahim said. 'I wonder why.'

I finished reading the manifesto. It was strong on anti-imperialist rhetoric, self-determination for Kashmir, land reform, and nationalization of industry, but far too soft on religion. I said I couldn't associate myself with a party that wasn't 100 per cent secular, and Rahim smiled in agreement, but Bhutto was angry and denounced us both. Later that evening, during dinner, I asked why he had embroiled the country in an unwinnable war. The reply was breathtaking: 'It was the only way to weaken the bloody dictatorship. The regime will crack wide open soon.'

Subsequent events appeared to vindicate Bhutto's judgement. In 1968, a prolonged uprising of students and workers finally toppled it. The traditional parties on the left had not grasped the importance of what was happening, but Bhutto put himself at the head of the revolt, promised that after the people's victory they would 'dress the generals in skirts and parade them through the streets like performing monkeys', and prospered politically.

When I met him in Karachi in August 1969, he was in an ebullient mood. The stopgap dictator had promised a general election, and Bhutto was sure his party would win. Once again he mocked me for refusing to join. 'There are only two ways: mine or Che Guevara's. Are you planning to start a guerrilla war in the mountains of Baluchistan?'

Bhutto scored an amazing triumph in the 1970 election, but only in West Pakistan. In what was then East Pakistan and is now Bangladesh, the nationalist leader Sheikh Mujibur Rahman and his Awami League won virtually every seat. Since 60 per cent of the population lived in East Pakistan, Mujibur gained an overall majority in the National Assembly and expected to become prime minister. The Punjabi elite refused to hand over power and instead arrested him. General Yahya ('fuck-fuck' in Lahori Punjabi) Khan attempted to crush the Bengalis, and Bhutto, desperate for power, supported him. It was his most shameful hour. A Bangladeshi government-in-exile was set up in neighbouring Calcutta. Millions of refugees poured into the Indian province of West Bengal, and finally, at the request of the Bengali leaders-in-exile, the Indian army moved into East Pakistan, to be greeted by the population as liberators. East Pakistan surrendered, and Bangladesh was born.

Bhutto came to power in a truncated Pakistan, but the old game was over: in 1972, at the Indian hill resort of Simla, he agreed to the status quo in Kashmir and in return got back the ninety thousand soldiers who had been captured after the fall of Dhaka, in what had been East Pakistan. In Kashmir, every political group, with the exception of the confessional Jamaat-e-Islami, was shocked by the brutalities inflicted on fellow Muslims in Bengal. Had a referendum been held at this point, a majority would have opted to remain within the Indian Federation, but Delhi refused to take the risk. Pakistan's reputation sank further when its third military dictator, the Washington implant Zia-ul-Haq, executed Bhutto in 1979 after a rigged trial. A large rally in Srinagar turned into a prayer meeting for the dead leader.

Sheikh Abdullah, who had been released from prison on grounds of ill-health in the mid-1970s, had made his peace with Delhi. In 1977 he was again appointed chief minister, courtesy of Mrs Gandhi, who forced Congress yes-men in the Kashmir Assembly, themselves elected by dubious means, to switch sides and vote for him. The changeover was calm: Kashmiris were pleased at Abdullah's return, but mindful of the fact that Mrs Gandhi was calling the tune.

Abdullah seemed stale and tired; his time in prison had affected both his health and his politics. He now mimicked other subcontinental potentates by attempting to create a political dynasty. It's said that Akbar Jehan insisted he do so and that he was too old and weak to resist. At a big rally in Srinagar he named his oldest son, Farooq Abdullah – an amiable doctor, fond of wine and fornication, but not very bright – as his successor.

As he lay dying, in 1982, Sheikh Abdullah told an old friend of a dream that had haunted him for thirty years: 'I am still a young man. I'm dressed as a bridegroom. I'm on horseback. My bridal party leaves our home with all the fanfare. We head in the direction of the bride's house. But when I arrive she's not there. She's never there. Then I wake up.' The missing bride, so it has always seemed to me, was Nehru. Abdullah had never fully recovered from his betrayal.

When I met Sheikh Abdullah's son Farooq at a conclave of opposition parties in Calcutta, he was scathing about Delhi's failures, but still convinced that a referendum would not go Pakistan's way. 'She's getting too old,' he said about Mrs Gandhi. 'Look at me. Who am I? In Indian terms, a nobody. A provincial politician. If she had left me alone there would have been no problems. Her congressmen in Kashmir were bitter at having been defeated, so they began to agitate, but for what? For power which the electorate had denied them. I met Mrs Gandhi a number of times to assure her that we were loyal, intended to remain so and wanted friendly relations with the centre. Her paranoia was such that she wanted one to be totally servile. That was impossible. So she gave the Kashmir Congress the green light to disrupt our government's functioning. It was she who made me a *national* leader. I would have been far happier left alone in our lovely Kashmir.'

When I passed this on to her, Mrs Gandhi snorted derisively. 'Yes, yes, I know that's what he *says*. He said similar things to me, but he acts differently. Tells too many lies. The boy is totally untrustworthy.' Meanwhile her 'sources' had informed her that Pakistan was preparing a military invasion of Kashmir. Could this be so? I doubted it. General Zia-ul-Haq was brutal and vicious, but he wasn't an idiot. He knew that to provoke India would be fatal. In addition, the Pakistan army was busy fighting the Soviet Union in Afghanistan.

To open a second front in Kashmir would be the height of irrationality.

'I'm surprised at you,' Mrs Gandhi said. 'You of all people believe that generals are rational human beings?'

'There is a difference between irrationality and suicide,' I said (a judgement I have since had cause to revise).

She smiled, but didn't reply. Then, to demonstrate the inadequacies of the military mind, she described how after Pakistan's surrender in Bangladesh her generals had wanted to continue the war against West Pakistan, to 'finish off the enemy'. She had overruled them and ordered a cease-fire. Her point was that in India the army was firmly under civilian control, but in Pakistan it was a law unto itself.

Later that evening – I was staying in Delhi – I received a phone call from a civil servant. 'I believe you had a very interesting discussion with the PM. We have an informal discussion club meeting tomorrow and would love you to come and talk to us.' The members of the club were civil servants, intelligence operatives and journalists from both the US and Soviet lobbies. They tried to convince me that I was wrong, that the Pakistani generals were planning an attack. After two hours of argument and counter-argument I began to tire. 'Listen,' I said, 'if you lot are preparing a pre-emptive strike against Zia or the nuclear reactor in Kahuta, that's your decision. You might even win support in Sind and Baluchistan, but don't expect the world to believe you acted in response to Pakistani aggression. It's simply not credible at the moment.' The meeting came to an end. Back in London I described these events to Bhutto's daughter, Benazir. 'Why did you deny that Zia was planning to invade Kashmir?' she interrupted.

Four months later, Mrs Gandhi was assassinated by her Sikh bodyguards. A civil servant I met in Delhi the following year

told me they had evidence linking the assassins with Sikh training camps in Pakistan that had been set up with US assistance
with a view to destabilizing the Indian government. He was
sure the United States had decided to eliminate Mrs Gandhi
in order to prevent a strike against Pakistan that would have
derailed the West's operation in Afghanistan. Bhutto had
certainly believed that Washington had orchestrated the coup
which toppled him. He smuggled out a testament from his
death cell which included Kissinger's threat to 'make a horri-
ble example' of him unless he desisted on the nuclear question. Many people in Bangladesh still insist that the CIA, using
the Saudis as a conduit, was responsible for Mujib's down-
fall. Mujib's daughter Haseena, currently prime minister of
Bangladesh, was out of the country at the time, and thus the
only member of the family to survive. The United States may
or may not have been involved, but it was a remarkable hat
trick: in the space of a decade, three populist politicians, each
hostile to US interests in the region, had been eliminated.

After the break-up of 1971, Pakistan appeared to lose interest
in Kashmir and South Asia as a whole. A young and ambitious
State Department official visited the country in 1980, a year
after Bhutto's execution, and advised Zia to look toward the
petrodollar surplus being accumulated by Saudi Arabia and the
Gulf states. Pakistan's large army was well positioned to guarantee the status quo in the Gulf. The Arabs would pay the bill.
Francis Fukuyama's position paper 'The Security of Pakistan:
A Trip Report' was taken very seriously by the military dictatorship. Officers and soldiers were dispatched to Riyadh and
Abu Dhabi to strengthen internal security. Salaries were much
higher there, and a posting to the Gulf was much sought after.
Pakistan also exported carefully selected prostitutes, recruited

from elite women's colleges. Islamic solidarity recognized no bounds.

With Islamabad's attention elsewhere, the Indian government could have reached an amicable settlement in Kashmir. But during the 1980s India interfered in the region with increasing ferocity, dismissing elected governments, imposing states of emergency, alternating soft and hard governors. Delhi's favourite despot, Jagmohan, was responsible for the suppression of the ultra-secular Jammu and Kashmir Liberation Front and the imprisonment and torture of its leader, Maqbool Bhat. Young Kashmiri men were arrested, tortured and killed by Indian soldiers; women of all ages were abused and raped. The aim was to break the will of the people, but instead many young men now took up arms, without bothering about where they came from.

I had met Bhat in Pakistani-controlled Kashmir in the early 1970s. He seemed equally hostile to Islamabad and New Delhi and determined to remake a Kashmir that would not be a helpless dependent of either. He was a great admirer of Che Guevara, and when I talked to him, in the euphoric aftermath of the 1969 uprising in Pakistan that had led to the fall of Ayub Khan, he was dreaming of a quick victory in Kashmir. I suggested that the rickety enthusiasm of a tiny minority was not enough. He reminded me that every revolutionary group (in Cuba, Vietnam, Algeria) had started off as a minority.

The Indian authorities arrested Bhat in 1976 and, charging him with the murder of a policeman, sentenced him to death. He was kept in prison as a bargaining counter until 1984, when he was executed in response to the kidnapping and murder of an Indian diplomat by Kashmiri militants in Birmingham. The vacuum he left would soon be filled by the men with beards, infiltrated, armed and funded by Pakistan.

By the late 1990s, after years of intra-Muslim factional violence, Afghanistan had come under the control of the Taliban – themselves funded, armed and sustained by the Pakistan army. Pakistan itself was in the grip of corrupt politicians, and sectarian in-fighting was claiming dozens of lives each month. In India, the Congress Party had lost its hold on national politics, paving the way for the Hindu fundamentalist BJP. In Kashmir, the number of armed Islamist groups multiplied as more and more veterans of the Afghan war came across the border to continue their fight for supremacy there. The main rivals were the indigenous Hizbul Mujahidin and the Pakistani-sponsored and armed Lashkar-i-Tayyaba and Harkatul Mujahidin. These groups killed each other's militants, kidnapped Western tourists, drove Kashmiri Hindus out of regions where they had lived for centuries, punished Kashmiri Muslims who remained stubbornly secular, and occasionally knocked off a few Indian soldiers and officials. Each group was willing, when convenient, to make terms with Delhi rather than combine with other groups to inflict punishment on the Indian government. Governor Jagmohan responded by making it as hard as he could for these Muslim groups to find new recruits. Night-long house-to-house searches became a part of everyday life. Young men were abducted by Indian soldiers, never to be seen again. In his self-serving memoir, *Frozen Turbulence*, Jagmohan explained: 'Obviously, I could not walk barefoot in a valley full of scorpions. I could leave nothing to chance.' The result of his policy was to win support for the gunmen.

Kashmir was ruled, more or less unhappily, by Delhi until 1996, when Farooq Abdullah came back to power – most of the other parties boycotted the elections. Since then, his collaboration with the BJP has destroyed his remaining reputation, and if a free election were permitted, his career as a politician would soon be over.

The Indian and Pakistan armies are among the largest in the world. In September 1998, the Pakistani high command decided to test Indian border defences in the virtually undefended Kargil-Drass region, a Himalayan wasteland fourteen thousand feet above sea level where Kashmir meets Pakistan and China. The region is one of mountain ridges and deep valleys, with temperatures averaging −20°C. It is also an area colonized by wild yellow roses, which bloom for a month each summer; the petals are eaten by villagers, who believe the rose nourishes the body and heals the soul. Most of the villagers are Shi'ite Muslims or Buddhists who live quiet, harmonious lives, sharing, among other things, an aversion to the Sunni fundamentalist imports from next door. The Pakistan army, whole-heartedly backed by Nawaz Sharif's government, crossed the Line of Control accompanied, just as it had been in 1947 and 1965, by soldiers disguised as irregulars and Lashkar-i-Tayyaba contingents, and occupied several ridges and villages. The Indian army moved troops to the area from Srinagar, and artillery duels became a daily nightmare for the locals.

Why had Pakistan embarked on an adventure of such obvious strategic futility? There was no possibility of triumphant entrances by victorious generals or politicians. Most Pakistani citizens, other than the Islamists, knew very little about what was happening in the mountains. Nor were they particularly interested in the fate of Kashmir. The real reasons for the war were ideological. Hafiz Mohammed Saeed, the head mullah of the Lashkar, told Pamela Constable of the *Washington Post*: 'Revenge is our religious duty. We beat the Russian superpower in Afghanistan; we can beat the Indian forces too. We fight with the help of Allah, and once we start jihad, no force can withstand us.' His argument was echoed by Pakistani officials. The Indians weren't as powerful as the Russians, and since they no longer possessed a nuclear monopoly in the region, there was no danger that a limited war would escalate. Second, and more important, Pakistan's actions would internationalize the conflict and bring the United States 'on side', as in Afghanistan and the Balkans.

In the war zone itself, India suffered initial reverses, then brought in more troops, helicopter gunships, and fighter jets, and began to bomb Pakistani installations across the border. If NATO could overfly borders without any legal sanction, so could they. By May 1999, as the yellow roses were about to bloom, the Indian army had retaken most of the ridges it had lost. A month later, its forces were poised to cross the Line of Control. Pakistan's political leaders panicked, and falling back on an old habit, they made a desperate appeal to the White House.

A US general was sent to Pakistan to have a quiet word with the military, and Nawaz Sharif was summoned to the White House. Clinton told him to withdraw all his troops, as well as the fundamentalists, from the territory they had occupied. Nothing was promised in return. No pressure on India. No money for Pakistan. Sharif capitulated. His information minister, Mushahid Hussain, had told the press just before the Washington visit that 'we did not start insurgency in Kashmir which is populous [*sic*], spontaneous and indigenous and we cannot stop it.' But they did. The dispute had indeed been internationalized, though not exactly as Pakistan had wanted. With China as the main enemy, Washington had dumped on Pakistan and was leaning heavily in India's direction.

In private, Sharif told the Americans that he supported a rapprochement with India and had resisted the Kargil war, but he had been outmanoeuvred by the army. The lie went down well in Washington and Delhi, but angered the Pakistani high command. When he got home, Sharif hatched a plan to replace the commander-in-chief of the army, General Pervaiz Musharraf, with one of his placemen, General Khwaja Ziaudin, head of the Inter-Services Intelligence (ISI). Sharif's brother Shahbaz made an unpublicized visit to Washington with Ziaudin in tow in order to get approval for Ziaudin's appointment. The two men were received at the White House, the Pentagon and the CIA and made many rash promises.

On 11 October 1999, while Musharraf was on his way back from a three-day official visit to Sri Lanka, Nawaz Sharif announced his dismissal and Ziaudin's promotion. The authorities at Karachi airport were instructed to divert the general's plane to a tiny airstrip in the interior of Sind, where he would be taken into custody. But the army refused to accept Ziaudin's authority, and the Karachi commander occupied the airport and ordered the plane to land. Musharraf was received with full military protocol. The army commander in the capital arrested the Sharif brothers and General Ziaudin. This was the first coup d'état carried out in the face of explicit American instructions to the contrary: in a statement issued three days before these events, Clinton had warned against a military take-over. In Pakistan, the fall of the Sharif brothers was celebrated on the streets of every city.

Musharraf pledged to wipe out corruption and restore standards in public life; in an unguarded interview he stressed his affinity with Kemal Ataturk, the founder of secular Turkey. No restrictions were placed on the press or political parties. Less than two years later, Musharraf's early anti-corruption zeal had dissipated. The fiercely incorruptible General Amjad was transferred from the Accountability Bureau to a military command in Karachi: he had amassed evidence revealing extensive corruption in every institution in the country. Supreme Court judges were for sale to the highest bidder (defence lawyers asked clients for six-figure sums as the 'judge's fee', payable before a trial began); many senior civil servants were on the payroll of big business and the narco-barons; businessmen pocketed bank loans worth billions of rupees; senior military officers had succumbed to bribery. Amjad insisted, to no avail, that the new regime clean up the armed forces. Unless retired and serving officers were tried, sentenced and punished, he believed, Pakistan would remain a failed state, dependent on foreign handouts and a black-market economy fuelled by narco-profits. His transfer shows that he lost this battle.

Many people in Pakistan had assumed that Musharraf would disarm the Islamists and restore a semblance of law and order in the big cities. Here, too, the regime made little progress, because it under-estimated Islamist penetration of the army. When I was in Lahore in December 1999, I was told about a disturbing incident. The Indians had informed their Pakistani counterparts that one of the peaks in Kargil-Drass was still occupied by Pakistani soldiers, contrary to the cease-fire agreement. A senior officer went to investigate and ordered the captain in charge of the peak to return to the Pakistani side of the Line of Control. The captain accused his senior officer and the military high command of betraying the Islamist cause, and shot the

officer dead. The Islamist officer was finally disarmed, tried by
a secret court martial and executed.

If, as is widely agreed, between 25 and 30 per cent of
Pakistan's soldiers are Islamists, the army's reluctance to act
against the jihadis is understandable: it is afraid of provoking
a civil war. Musharraf has a serious problem – and it's not just
his problem. The fundamentalists' boast that in ten years' time
they will control the army and hence Pakistan conjures a deadly
image: an Islamist finger on the nuclear trigger. This is what has
concentrated minds in Washington, Delhi and Beijing, but so
far with little to show for it.

Neither Pakistan nor India favours the cause of Kashmiri
independence. Nor does Beijing, worried about the ramifi-
cations in Tibet. And yet independence is what the Kashmiri
people appear to want. In the valley itself, Farooq Abdullah
and his BJP chums, backed by Karan Singh, are plotting a
Balkanization of the province, dividing it into eight units along
religious–ethnic lines. The J&K Liberation Front, meanwhile,
has published a map showing its favoured boundaries for an
independent Kashmir, made up of territory currently occupied by India, Pakistan and China. Hashim Qureshi, one of the
leaders of the organization, told me that they did not want all
the paraphernalia of a modern state. They weren't interested
in having an army. They would be happy for their frontiers to
be guaranteed by China, India and Pakistan, so that Kashmir,
the cause of three wars, could become a secular, multicultural
paradise, open to citizens of both India and Pakistan. At the
moment this is a noble, but utopian, hope. The political land-
scape is exceptionally bleak. (A pamphlet issued by a jihadi
group in Pakistan in 2002 called for donations to fund the struggle: the total launch fee for a jihad is 140,000 rupees; the price

of a Kalashnikov is given as Rs 20,000; a single bullet is Rs 35; a Kenwood wireless is Rs 28,000.)

For the people who live here, 11 September did not change anything. The Jaish-e-Muhammad group carried out a brutal terrorist act in Srinagar days later. More than forty people were killed. It is the same group that, a few weeks later, killed a group of Christians in the Pakistani city of Bahawalpur. The reason this group cannot be disarmed is that it is a creation of Pakistani military intelligence. The links between official and unofficial are inextricable. In retaliation, India bombed a few targets inside Pakistani territory. The message was obvious. If the West can inflict punitive bombing on Afghanistan, then India can do the same to Pakistan. The terrorist attack on the Indian Parliament by one of these groups in December 2001 almost led to a war between the two countries. Pakistan acted against the leaders of the fundamentalist armies, but the membership has ominously disappeared.

The chapter of South Asian history that opened with the Partition of 1947 needs to be closed. Most people want a durable peace. There are now three large states in the region: India, Pakistan and Bangladesh, with a combined population of well over a billion human beings. On the periphery are Nepal, Bhutan and Sri Lanka. Linguistically diverse, the region shares a culture and a history in common. Economic and political logic dictates the formation of a South Asian Union, a voluntary confederation of republics. Within such a framework, in which no state fears a challenge to its sovereignty, Kashmir could be guaranteed complete autonomy, as could the Tamil region in Sri Lanka. Shared sovereignty is better than none at all. A massive reduction in military expenditure and trade deals with China and the Far Eastern bloc could even benefit the continent as a whole. The Empire prefers to play the role of supreme arbiter these days, but its solutions put its own interests first. It would make much more sense for the South Asian states and China to forgo its mediation of the Empire and speak with each other directly. If they fail to do so, they might discover, sometime later this century, that beneath the benign gaze of the Empire, the forces of rampant capitalism are breaking up both China and India. Now there's a thought.

Arundhati Roy

A*ʐadi*: The Only Thing Kashmiris Want

In 2008, the Kashmiri struggle for freedom, azadi, *entered a new phase with the most widespread and sustained mass uprising in over a decade. Arundhati Roy was there for that first summer of discontent, the events of which have been repeated each year since.*

During the summer months of 2008, the people of Kashmir were free. Free in the most profound sense. They shrugged off the terror of living their lives in the gun-sights of half a million heavily armed soldiers in the most densely militarized zone in the world.

After eighteen years of administering a military occupation, the Indian government found its worst nightmare had come true. Having declared that Kashmir's militant movement had been crushed, it was faced with a non-violent mass protest, but not the kind it knows how to manage. This one was nourished by people's memory of years of repression in which tens of thousands had been killed, thousands had been 'disappeared', and hundreds of thousands had been tortured, injured, raped and humiliated. That kind of rage, once it finds expression, cannot easily be tamed, re-bottled and sent back to where it came from.

For all those years, the Indian state, known amongst the knowing as the Deep State, had done everything it could to subvert, suppress, represent, misrepresent, discredit, interpret, intimidate, purchase, and simply snuff out the voice of the Kashmiri people. It had used money (lots of it), violence (lots of it), disinformation, propaganda, torture, elaborate networks of collaborators and informers, terror, imprisonment, blackmail and rigged elections to subdue what democrats would call the will of the people. But the Deep State, as deep states eventually tend to do, tripped on its own hubris and bought into its own publicity. It made the mistake of believing that domination was victory, that the 'normalcy' it had enforced through the barrel of a gun was indeed normal, and that the people's sullen silence was acquiescence.

The well-endowed peace industry, speaking on the people's behalf, informed us that 'Kashmiris are tired of violence and want peace.' What kind of peace they were willing to settle for was never clarified. Bollywood's cache of Kashmir/Muslim-terrorist films had brainwashed most Indians into believing that all of Kashmir's sorrows could be laid at the door of evil, people-hating terrorists.

To anybody who cared to ask, or, more importantly, to *listen*, it was always clear that even in their darkest moments, people in Kashmir had kept the fires burning and that it was not only peace they yearned for, but freedom too.

In a sudden twist of fate, an ill-conceived move over the transfer of a hundred acres of state forest-land to the Amarnath Shrine Board (which manages the annual Hindu pilgrimage to a cave deep in the Kashmir Himalayas) became the equivalent of a lit match tossed into a barrel of petrol. Until 1989, the Amarnath pilgrimage attracted about 20,000 people, who travelled to the Amarnath cave over a period of about two weeks. In 1990, when the overtly Islamic militant uprising in the Kashmir

Valley coincided with the spread of virulent Hindutva (Hindu nationalism) in the Indian plains, the number of pilgrims began to increase exponentially. By 2008, more than 500,000 pilgrims were visiting the Amarnath cave annually, travelling in large groups, their passage often sponsored by Indian business houses.

To many people in the valley, this dramatic increase in numbers was seen as an aggressive political statement by an increasingly Hindu-fundamentalist Indian state. Rightly or wrongly, the land transfer was viewed as the thin edge of the wedge. It triggered an anxiety: that this was the beginning of an elaborate plan to build Israeli-style settlements and change the demographics of the valley.

Days of massive protest forced the valley to shut down completely. Within hours, the protests spread from the cities to villages. Young stone-throwers took to the streets and faced armed police, who fired straight at them, killing several. For the Kashmiri people as well as the Indian government, this uprising resurrected memories of the uprising in the early 1990s. Throughout the weeks of protest, hartal (general strikes) and police violence, the Hindutva publicity machine charged Kashmiris with committing every kind of communal excess, while the 500,000 Amarnath pilgrims completed their pilgrimage not only unhurt, but also touched by the hospitality they had been shown by local people.

Eventually, having been taken completely by surprise by the ferocity of the response, the government revoked the land transfer. But by then the land transfer had become what senior separatist leader Syed Ali Shah Geelani called a non-issue.

Massive protests against the revocation erupted in the predominantly Hindu city of Jammu. There, too, the issue snowballed into something much bigger. Hindus began to raise issues of neglect and discrimination by the Indian state. (For some odd reason they blamed Kashmiris for that neglect.) The protests led to the blockading of the Jammu–Srinagar highway, the only functional road link between Kashmir and India. The army was called out to clear the highway and allow safe passage of trucks between Jammu and Srinagar. But incidents of violence against Kashmiri truckers were being reported from as far away as Punjab, where there was no protection at all. As a result, Kashmiri truckers, fearing for their lives, refused to drive on the highway. Truckloads of perishable fresh fruit and valley produce began to rot. It became very obvious that the blockade had caused the situation to spin out of control. The government announced that the blockade had been cleared and that trucks were going through. Sections of the Indian media, quoting the inevitable 'intelligence' sources, began to refer to it as a 'perceived' blockade, and even to suggest that there had never been one.

But it was too late for those games; the damage had been done. It had been demonstrated in no uncertain terms to people in Kashmir that they lived on sufferance and that if they didn't behave themselves they could be put under siege, starved, deprived of essential commodities and medical supplies. The real blockade became a psychological one. The last fragile link between India and Kashmir had all but snapped.

To expect matters to end there was, of course, absurd. Hadn't anybody noticed that in Kashmir even minor protests about civic issues like water and electricity inevitably turned into demands for *azadi*? To threaten them with mass starvation amounted to committing political suicide.

Not surprisingly, the voice that the Government of India tried so hard to silence in Kashmir massed into a deafening roar.

Hundreds of thousands of unarmed people came out to reclaim their cities, their streets and mohallas (neighbourhoods). They simply overwhelmed the heavily armed security forces by their sheer numbers, and by a remarkable display of raw courage.

Raised in a playground of army camps, check-points, and bunkers, with screams from torture chambers for a sound track, the younger generation suddenly discovered the power of mass protest, and above all the dignity of being able to straighten their shoulders and speak for themselves, represent themselves. For them, it was nothing short of an epiphany. In full flow, not even the fear of death seemed to hold them back. And once that fear has gone, of what use is the largest, or second-largest, army in the world? What threat does it hold? Who knows this better than the people of India, who won their independence in the way that they did?

The circumstances in Kashmir being what they were, it was hard for the spin doctors to fall back on the same old, same old – to claim that it was all the doing of Pakistan's Inter-Services Intelligence (ISI), or that people were being coerced by militants. Since the 1930s onwards, the question of who can claim the right to represent that elusive thing known as Kashmiri sentiment has been bitterly contested. Was it Sheikh Abdullah? The Muslim Conference? Who is it today? The mainstream political parties? The Hurriyat? The militants? But this time around, the people were in charge. There had been mass rallies in the past, but none in recent memory had been so sustained and widespread.

The mainstream political parties of Kashmir – the National Conference, the People's Democratic Party – fêted by the Deep State and the Indian media, despite the pathetic voter turnout in election after election, appeared dutifully for debates in New

Delhi's TV studios but couldn't muster the courage to appear on the streets of Kashmir. Through the worst years of oppression, the armed militants had been seen as the only ones carrying the torch of *azadi* forward. But in 2008, if they were around at all, they seemed to be content to take a back seat and let the people do the fighting for a change.

The separatist leaders who did appear to speak at the rallies have not been leaders so much as *followers*, guided by the phenomenal spontaneous energy of a caged, enraged people, energy that exploded on Kashmir's streets. These leaders, such as they are, were being presented with a full-blown revolution. The only condition seemed to be that they do as the people said. If they said things that people did not wish to hear, they were gently persuaded to come out, publicly apologize, and correct their course. This applied to all of them, including Syed Ali Shah Geelani, who at one public rally proclaimed himself the movement's only leader. It was a monumental political blunder that very nearly shattered the fragile new alliance between the various factions of the struggle. Within hours he retracted his statement. Like it or not, this is democracy. No democrat could pretend otherwise.

Day after day, hundreds of thousands of people swarmed around places that held terrible memories for them. They demolished bunkers, broke through cordons of concertina wire and stared straight down the barrels of the soldiers' machine guns, saying what very few in India want to hear: '*Hum kya chahte? Azadi!*' We Want Freedom. And, it has to be said, they shouted in equal numbers and with equal intensity, '*Jeevey jeevey Pakistan!*' Long live Pakistan!

That sound reverberated through the valley like the drumbeat of steady rain on a tin roof, or like the roll of thunder before an electric storm. It was the plebiscite that was never held, the referendum that has been indefinitely postponed.

On 15 August, India's Independence Day, the city of Srinagar shut down completely. The Bakshi stadium, where Governor N. N. Vohra hoisted the Indian flag, was empty except for a few officials. Hours later, Lal Chowk, the nerve centre of the city (where, in 1992, Murli Manohar Joshi, leader of the Bharatiya Janata Party (BJP) and mentor of the controversial 'Hinduization' of children's history textbooks, had started a tradition of flag-hoisting by the Border Security Force), was taken over by thousands of people who hoisted the Pakistani flag and wished each other 'Happy belated Independence Day' (Pakistan celebrates Independence on 14 August) and 'Happy Slavery Day'. Humour, obviously, has survived India's many torture centres and Abu Ghraibs in Kashmir.

On 16 August, more than 300,000 people marched to Pampore, to the village of Hurriyat leader Sheikh Abdul Aziz, who was shot down in cold blood five days earlier. He had been part of a massive march to the Line of Control demanding that since the Jammu road had been blocked, it was only logical that the Srinagar–Muzaffarabad highway be opened for goods and people, the way it used to be before Kashmir was partitioned.

On 18 August, an equal number gathered in Srinagar on the vast grounds of the TRC (Tourist Reception Centre, not the Truth and Reconciliation Committee), close to the United Nations Military Observers Group in India and Pakistan (UNMOGIP), to submit a memorandum asking for three things: the end to Indian rule, the deployment of a UN peace-keeping force, and an investigation into two decades of war crimes committed with almost complete impunity by the Indian army and police.

The day before the rally the Deep State was hard at work. A senior journalist friend called me to say that late in the afternoon the home secretary had called a high-level meeting in New Delhi. Also present were the defence secretary and the intelligence chiefs. The purpose of the meeting, he said, was to brief the editors of TV news channels that the government had reason to believe that the insurrection was being managed by a small splinter cell of the ISI and to request that the news channels keep this piece of exclusive, highly secret intelligence in mind while covering (or preferably not covering?) the news from Kashmir. Unfortunately for the Deep State, things had gone so far that the TV stations, had they obeyed those instructions, would have run the risk of looking ridiculous. Thankfully, the revolution would, after all, be televised.

On the night of 17 August, the police sealed the city. Streets were barricaded; thousands of armed police manned the barriers. The roads leading into Srinagar were blocked. For the first time in eighteen years, the police had to plead with Hurriyat leaders to address the rally at the TRC grounds instead of marching right up to the UNMOGIP office, which is on Gupkar Road, Srinagar's Green Zone, where for years the Indian establishment has barricaded itself in style and splendour.

On the morning of the 18th, people began pouring into Srinagar from villages and towns across the valley. In trucks, Tempos, jeeps, buses, and on foot. Once again, barriers were broken and people reclaimed their city. The police were faced with the choice of either stepping aside or executing a massacre. They stepped aside. Not a single bullet was fired.

The city floated on a sea of smiles. There was ecstasy in the air. Everyone had a banner: houseboat owners, traders, students, lawyers, doctors. One said, 'We are all prisoners, set us free.' Another said, 'Democracy without freedom is Demon-crazy.' Demon Crazy. That was a good one. Perhaps he was referring to the twisted logic of a country that needed to commit communal carnage in order to bolster its secular credentials. Or the insanity that permits the world's largest democracy to administer the world's largest military occupation and continue to call itself a democracy.

There was a green flag on every lamp-post, every roof, every bus stop, and on the tops of chinar trees. A big one fluttered outside the All India Radio building. Road signs to Hazratbal, Batmaloo, Sopore were painted over. *Rawalpindi*, they said. Or simply, *Pakistan*.

It would be a mistake to assume that the public expression of affection for Pakistan automatically translates into a desire to accede to Pakistan. Some of it has to do with gratitude for the support – cynical or otherwise – for what Kashmiris see as a freedom struggle and the Indian state sees as a terrorist campaign. It also has to do with mischief. With saying and doing what galls India, the enemy, most of all. (It's easy to scoff at the idea of a 'freedom struggle' that wishes to distance itself from a country that is supposed to be a democracy and align itself with another that has been ruled, for the most part, by military dictators. A country whose army committed genocide in what is now Bangladesh. A country that is even now being torn apart by its own ethnic war. These are important questions, but right now, perhaps it's more useful to wonder what the so-called democracy did in Kashmir to make people hate it so.)

Everywhere there were Pakistani flags, everywhere the cry *Pakistan se rishta kya? La ilaha illallah.* What is our bond with Pakistan? There is no god but Allah. *Azadi ka matlab kya? La ilaha illallah*. What does freedom mean? There is no god but Allah.

For somebody like myself, who is not Muslim, that interpretation of freedom is hard – if not impossible – to understand. I asked a young woman whether freedom for Kashmir would not mean less freedom for her, as a woman. She shrugged and said, 'What kind of freedom do we have now? The freedom to be raped by Indian soldiers?' Her reply silenced me.

Standing on the grounds of the TRC, surrounded by a sea of green flags, I found it impossible to doubt or ignore the deeply Islamic nature of the uprising taking place around me, and equally impossible to label it a vicious, terrorist jihad. For Kashmiris, it was a catharsis. A historical moment in a long and complicated struggle for freedom with all the imperfections, cruelties and confusions that freedom, struggles have. This one cannot by any means call itself pristine, and it will always be stigmatized by, and will some day, I hope, have to account for – among other things – the brutal killings of Kashmiri Pandits in the early years of the uprising, culminating in the exodus of almost the entire community from the Kashmir Valley.

As the crowd continued to swell, I listened carefully to the slogans, because rhetoric often clarifies things and holds the key to all kinds of understanding. I'd heard many of them already, a few years before, at a militant's funeral. A new one, obviously coined after the blockade, was *Kashmir ki mandi! Rawalpindi!* (It doesn't lend itself to translation, but it means: Kashmir's marketplace? Rawalpindi!) Another was *Khooni lakir tod do, aar paar jod do* (Break down the blood-soaked Line of Control; let Kashmir be united again). There were plenty of insults and humiliation for India: *Ay jabiron ay zalimon, Kashmir hamara chhod do* (O oppressors, O wicked ones, get out of our Kashmir). *Jis Kashmir ko khoon se seencha, woh Kashmir hamara hai!* (The Kashmir we have irrigated with our blood, that Kashmir is ours!).

The slogan that cut through me like a knife and clean broke my heart was this one: *Nanga bhookha Hindustan, jaan se pyaara Pakistan* (Naked, starving India, more precious than life itself— Pakistan). Why was it so galling, so painful to listen to this? I tried to work it out and settled on three reasons. First, because we all know that the first part of the slogan is the embarrassing and unadorned truth about India, the emerging superpower. Second, because all Indians who are not *nanga* or *bhookha* are – and have been – complicit in complex and historical ways in the cultural and economic systems that make Indian society so cruel, so vulgarly unequal.

And third, because it was painful to listen to people who have suffered so much themselves mock others who suffer in different ways, but no less intensely, under the same oppressor. In that slogan I saw the seeds of how easily victims can become perpetrators.

It took hours for Mirwaiz Umer Farooq (the chairman of Hurriyat) and Syed Ali Shah Geelani to wade through the thronging crowds and make it onto the podium. When they arrived, they were borne aloft on the shoulders of young men, over the surging crowd. The roar of greeting was deafening. Mirwaiz Umer spoke first. He repeated the demand that the Armed Forces Special Powers Act, Disturbed Areas Act and Public Safety Act – under which thousands have been killed, jailed, and tortured – be revoked. He called for the release of political prisoners, for the Srinagar–Muzaffarabad road to be opened for the free movement of goods and people, and for the demilitarization of the Kashmir Valley.

Syed Ali Shah Geelani began his address with a recitation from the Quran. He then said what he has said before, on hundreds of occasions. The only way for the struggle to succeed, he said, was to turn to the Quran for guidance. He said that Islam would guide the struggle and that it was a complete social and moral code that would govern the people of a free Kashmir. He said that Pakistan had been created as the home of Islam, and that that goal should never be subverted. He said that just as Pakistan belonged to Kashmir, Kashmir belonged to Pakistan. He said that minority communities would have full rights and their places of worship would be safe. Each point he made was applauded.

Oddly enough, the apparent doctrinal clarity of what he said made everything a little unclear. I wondered how the somewhat disparate views of the various factions in the freedom struggle would resolve themselves – the Jammu and Kashmir Liberation Front's vision of an independent state, Geelani's desire to merge with Pakistan, and Mirwaiz Umer Farooq balanced precariously between them.

An old man with a red eye standing next to me said, 'Kashmir was one country. Half was taken by India, the other half by Pakistan. Both by force. We want freedom.' I wondered if, in the new dispensation, the old man would get a hearing. I wondered what he would think of the trucks that roared down the highways in the plains of India, owned and driven by men who knew nothing of history, or of Kashmir, but still had slogans on their tail-gates that said, '*Doodh maango to kheer denge; Kashmir maango to cheer denge*' (Ask for milk, you'll get cream; ask for Kashmir, we'll tear you open).

Briefly, I had another thought. I imagined myself standing in the heart of a Rashtriya Swayasevak Sangh or Vishva Hindu Parishad rally being addressed by L. K. Advani (then president of the BJP). Replace the word *Islam* with the word *Hindutva*, replace the word *Pakistan* with *Hindustan*, replace the sea of green flags with saffron ones, and we would have the BJP's nightmare vision of an ideal India.

Is that what we should accept as our future? Monolithic religious states handing down a complete social and moral code, 'a complete way of life'? Millions of us in India reject the Hindutva project. Our rejection springs from love, from passion, from a kind of idealism, from having an enormous emotional stake in the society in which we live. What our neighbours do, how they choose to handle their affairs, does not diminish but strengthens our argument.

Arguments that spring from love are also fraught with danger. It is for the people of Kashmir to agree or disagree with the Islamic project (which is as much contested, in equally complex ways, by Muslims all over the world as Hindutva is contested by Hindus). It is time for those who are part of the struggle to outline a vision for what kind of society they are fighting for. It is time to offer people something more than martyrs, slogans, and vague generalizations. Those who wish to turn to the Quran for guidance will no doubt find guidance there. But what of those who do not wish to do that, or for whom the Quran does not make a place? Do the Hindus of Jammu and other minorities also have the right to self-determination? Will the hundreds of thousands of Kashmiri Pandits now living in exile, many of them in terrible poverty, have the right to return? Will they be paid reparations for the terrible losses they have suffered? Or will a free Kashmir do to its minorities what India has done to

Kashmiris for sixty-three years? What will happen to homosexuals and adulterers and blasphemers? What of thieves and *lafangas* and writers who do not agree with the 'complete social and moral code'? Will we be put to death as we are in Saudi Arabia? Will the cycle of death, repression and bloodshed continue? History offers many models for Kashmir's thinkers and intellectuals and politicians to study. What will the Kashmir of their dreams look like? Algeria? Iran? South Africa? Switzerland? Pakistan?

In liberation struggles, few things are more important than dreams. A lazy utopia and a flawed sense of justice will have consequences that do not bear thinking about. This is not the time for intellectual sloth or a reluctance to assess a situation clearly and honestly. It could be argued that the prevarication of Maharaja Hari Singh in 1947 has been Kashmir's great modern tragedy, one that eventually led to unthinkable bloodshed and the prolonged bondage of people who were very nearly free.

In 2008, the spectre of partition quickly reared its head. Hindutva networks were alive with rumours about Hindus in the valley being attacked and forced to flee. In response, phone calls from Jammu reported that an armed Hindu militia was threatening a massacre and that Muslims from the two Hindu majority districts were preparing to flee. (Memories of the bloodbath that ensued and claimed the lives of more than a million people when India and Pakistan were partitioned have come flooding back. That nightmare will haunt all of us forever.)

There is absolutely no reason to believe that history will repeat itself. Not unless it is made to. Not unless people actively work to create such a cataclysm.

However, none of these fears of what the future holds can justify the continued military occupation of a nation and a people. No more than the old colonial argument about how the natives were not ready for freedom justified the colonial project.

Of course there are many ways for the Indian state to continue to hold on to Kashmir. It could do what it does best. Wait. And hope that the people's energy will dissipate in the absence of a concrete plan. It could try to fracture the fragile coalition that is emerging. It could extinguish the non-violent uprisings and reinvite armed militancy. It could increase the number of troops from half a million to a million. A few strategic massacres, a couple of targeted assassinations, some disappearances and a massive round of arrests should do the trick for a few more years.

The unimaginable amount of public money that are needed to keep the military occupation of Kashmir going is money that ought by right to be spent on schools and hospitals and food for an impoverished, malnourished population in India. What kind of government can possibly believe that it has the right to spend that money on more weapons, more concertina wire and more prisons in Kashmir?

The Indian military occupation of Kashmir makes monsters of us all. It allows Hindu chauvinists to target and victimize Muslims in India by holding them hostage to the freedom struggle being waged by Muslims in Kashmir. It's all being stirred into a poisonous brew and administered intravenously, straight into our bloodstream.

At the heart of it all is a moral question. Does any government have the right to take away people's liberty with military force?

India needs *azadi* from Kashmir just as much – if not more – than Kashmir needs *azadi* from India.

Habba Khatun

Poems by a Queen of Kashmir

Translated by Nilla Cram Crook

Habba Khatun

I left my home for play
Nor yet again
Returned, although the day
Sank in the West.
The name I made is hailed
On lips of men,
Habba Khatun! Though veiled,
I found no rest.
Through crowds I found my way,
From forests, then,
The sages came, when day
Sank in the West.

Lol of the Lonely Pine

The one who dazzles – have you seen that one?
Upon him look!
A sleepless stream, in search of him I run,
A restless brook.
In far-off woods, a lonely pine I stood
Till he appeared,
My woodcutter, and came to cut the wood.
His fire I feared,
Yet though he burn my logs, behold, I shine,
My ashes wine!

Never Return These Hours

Meadows I cover with flowers for you,
Come, my lover of flowers!
Come, let me gather fresh jasmine for you,
Never return these hours!
Lilacs have bloomed by the river for you,
Deeply the world is asleep,
Still, though, no answer has reached me from you,
Garlands of green I keep.
What if they speak only evil of me?
Who has been able to change destiny?
Come, my lover of flowers!

Song of the Restless Stream

The world its Ramadan will end,
The lover's Eid,

The feast of love, O call him, friend!
For love is Eid.

But love has melted me like snow,
A waterfall,
As restless as the summer streams
I sleepless go!

O, call him gently, friend, O call!
With wreaths and dreams
I carry wine to Dara's peaks
The world below.

And yet he roams in distant vales.
New wine he seeks!
If he comes not, the jasmine pales,
And I, and all!

Gather Violets, O Narcissus!

Rain has come, and fields and fruit trees sing,
Spring has come, and Love, the Lord of Spring,
Dandelions have lifted up their faces,
Cold has gone and every wintry thing!
Forget-me-not the forest graces,
Iris and the lily spring will bring.
Gather violets, O Narcissus,
Winter's ashes from our door I fling!
The water-bird the lake embraces,
How can frost upon your petals cling?

The Golden Wine Cups of the Night

In henna I have dyed my hands,
When will he come?
I die, while he roams distant lands,
My heart is numb!

O, where is now the day's delight?
I've waited long.
The golden wine cups of the night
To him belong!

The ritual of love is sweet,
Could I adorn
My love with jewels, perfume his feet,
Be no more torn,

Anoint him with my fragrant kiss,
Love, for your sake,
The lotus of my heart in bliss
Would block the lake!

Lol of the Wild Yellow Rose

Wild, the vagrant yellow rose
Again has bloomed,
Beauty has in all that grows
Rare forms assumed!
Where, O love, your hiding place?
I wander far,
Seeking you among the streams

The dew-drops pour.
Jasmine in the forest gleams,
But where your face?
Violets bloom for me to trace
To where you are.

Why Are You Cross with Me?

Which rival of mine has lured you away from me?
Why are you cross with me?
Forget the anger and the sulkiness,
You are my only love,
Why are you cross with me?
My garden has blossomed into colourful flowers,
Why are you away from me?
My love, my only love, I think only of you,
Why are you cross with me?
I kept my doors open half the night,
Come and enter my door, my jewel,
Why have you forsaken the path to my house?
Why are you cross with me?
I swear, my love, I am waiting for you,
Dressed in colourful robes,
My youth is in full bloom now,
Why are you cross with me?
Oh, marksman, my bosom is open
To the darts you throw at me.
These darts are piercing me,
Why are you cross with me?
I have been wasting away like snow is summer heat.
My youth is in its bloom.

This is your garden, come and enjoy it.
Why are you cross with me?
I have sought you over hills and dales,
I have sought you from dawn till dusk,
I have cooked dainty dishes for you,
I am pining for you,
What is my fault, O my love?
Why don't you seek me out?
Why are cross with me?
The shock of your desertion has come as a blow to me,
O cruel one, I continue to nurse the pain.
Why are you cross with me?
I have not complained even to the spring breeze
That is my agony.
Why have you forgotten me?
Who will take care of me?

Why are you cross with me?
I swear by you I do not go out at all,
I don't even show up at the spring.
My body is burning,
Why don't you soothe it?
Why are you cross with me?
My hurt is marrow deep; I did not complain.
I just wasted away for you.
I have suppressed endless longing,
Why are you cross with me?
I, Habba Khatun, am grieving now.
Why didn't I ever greet you, my love?
The day is fading and I keep recalling,
Why are you cross with me?

Hilal Bhatt

Fayazabad 31223

Nineteen eighty-seven, the year I finished fifth grade, was a watershed year in the history of my homeland, Kashmir. It was the first and last year that my countrymen in Indian-administered Kashmir participated en masse in an assembly election with dreams of having their own government.

I would finish school at four o'clock, hurry home and then leave with other children from my village in South Kashmir to attend a Muslim United Front rally. MUF was a coalition of independent, local political parties that had decided to contest elections in opposition to the candidates of the parties beholden to New Delhi: the National Conference and the Congress.

Many who would go on to become separatists and even militants, like Syed Salhauddin (now chief of the United Jihad Council, an alliance of Islamic armed resistance groups), had come together to establish a people's government in the state.

Even prior to the ill-fated elections of 1987, there had been a widespread belief among the people of Kashmir that they had never been given a fair chance to choose their own representatives: since the first such elections, in 1951, the ruling parties had always been those backed by New Delhi. A section of the Kashmiri leadership had always boycotted the elections, demanding the implementation of the 1948 UN resolution for a plebiscite in Kashmir on self-determination. Now, the MUF saw the 1987 elections as a route to the plebiscite.

The emergence of the Muslim United Front rekindled confidence in the democratic process. People overwhelmingly supported the MUF candidates. Kashmir looked even greener with its streets, bazaars, rooftops and roads painted the colour of the MUF flag. It was the highest turnout ever for a Kashmir assembly election. But the results disappointed everyone. Of the forty-four seats the MUF contested, it won four, while the National Conference–Congress alliance took sixty-six. Accounts of how officials had rigged the count and replaced the ballot boxes became household stories. Children from the age of fourteen up began recruiting themselves as cadres of the Liberation Front, Hizbul Mujahidin, Al-Ummar, and other indigenous guerrilla organizations.

Groups of about a dozen boys would cross the border into Pakistan, receive training in guerrilla warfare, and return to Kashmir to fight Indian rule. Every day we heard news of more children joining these groups and heading toward the frontier districts of Kupwara and Baramulla, where they crossed the Line of Control (LOC), the de facto border between Indian- and Pakistani-held territories in Kashmir. Children at my school longed for their turn to become militants, heroes.

The principal of our school, a tall, wiry man in his early forties with a strand of long beard on his chin, was a Jammat-e-Islami sympathizer. I still remember the day when, in class, he declared that he had lost all hope in India and asked the students to prepare for an armed rebellion: 'You saw what happened in the assembly election. India will never let us enjoy even a basic right like choosing our own representatives. Kashmir is occupied. Peace and dignity can only prevail through the barrel of the gun.' That was the last lesson he taught in the classroom.

Barely a week later, the news that the principal had crossed the LOC was confirmed when his name figured among a group of Muzaffarabad-based Kashmiris who had requested a Kashmiri song on the Radio Kashmir station there and dedicated it to his friends on our side of the Line of Control. Families parted by the LOC would frequently send messages to their friends and relatives through Azad Kashmir radio. For that reason it was a popular station in both parts of Kashmir. It became even more popular after the 1987 elections.

We learned that our principal had also taken with him his fourteen-year-old son and three other boys from the ninth grade to be trained in guerrilla warfare. The news put a bee in our school bonnet. My classmates all produced two versions of the essay 'My Aim in Life'. The first version was for our Pandit teacher, Somnath; the second was our principal's last lesson turned into a personal declaration.

During recess we would often sit in the apple orchard adjacent to our school and share our secret versions of this essay. Without exception, everybody in our class, including the girls, wanted to become mujahidin – fighters.

A year later, the boys who had crossed the LOC returned. They made their presence felt, firing indiscriminately on the Indian army convoys that would routinely pass along the nearby National Highway 1-A, which connected Srinagar with Jammu. The boys occasionally planted improvised explosive devices and land-mines under the highway culverts. Every time an *action* – our local term for an attack on an army convoy – occurred, masses of people would flee the villages before the army could come and look for the boys who'd undertaken it.

The soldiers would barge into the houses and beat the children. The next day, more boys would vow to cross the border and become fighters.

During our annual school exams, boys stood guard at the exam hall with pistols hidden in their pockets. They made sure nobody was copying or cheating and kept an eye on a few exam invigilators who were notorious for taking money from students for helping them to pass the grade.

Students who repeatedly failed the annual exam found it easier to gain standing in the village if they embraced the gun and became militant. One of them, Shabir, went to Muzaffarabad before the tenth grade annual exam and returned three years later with the largest gun I had ever seen.

The boys would often pass through the villages with their guns hidden in their *phirens,* the long woollen gowns Kashmiris wear in the winter. My classmates loved narrating the previous night's story of spotting militants with Kalashnikovs.

At nightfall, the militants would stop and enter a village house, spend the night there and start their journey before dawn the next day. Occasionally they walked in large groups, with guns of different shapes and sizes slung over their shoulders.

Late one evening in 1989, when I was in the seventh grade, two boys jumped the brick wall around our house and came in through the kitchen door. We stood scared as they took their AK-47 rifles out of their *phirens* and placed them under the bulky walnut bed which dominated the drawing room.

My mother prepared dinner for them. They ate, offered prayers and slept. None of us were able to sleep. In the middle of the night, I was surprised to see my father smoking by the window that overlooked the village road. I was worried about the possibility of soldiers cordoning off the house and exchanging fire with our guests. But I was more excited about the AK-47s that were lying beneath the walnut bed in the drawing room. I wanted to touch one. Feel it in my hands. Pull the trigger and experience the force. I wanted to tell my classmates just how forceful a real AK-47 was.

I woke up early in the morning and sneaked into the drawing room. The boys were in a deep sleep. I went to the bed, got hold of a rifle and hid it beneath my *phiren*. Before I opened the door, I looked back to check that they had not seen me and then I left the house, heading toward the open fields outside the village, Kalashnikov in hand. A strange energy took over my body. With the gun in my *phiren*, my tread became heavier, firmer, like an adult's. I walked fearlessly past the men waiting for early morning bread at the village bakery.

I crossed the cemented embankment of the spring on the village periphery, where women and young girls would assemble early in the morning to wash their dishes and gossip about village boys. Half a mile on, I got to an open mustard field near the village tableland, looked back, and convinced myself there was nobody around. I took the rifle out of my *phiren*, looked at it and took a deep breath. Before I could pull the trigger and experience the force, my father came from behind, slapped me and took the gun.

Fearing that their children would go across the border to become militants, many parents had begun sending them to schools outside the valley. Two years after the AK-47 incident, my parents followed suit.

After finishing eighth grade, in 1991, I was sent to Minto Circle School, along with seven fellow Kashmiris. The pioneering educationist Sir Syed Ahmed Khan had founded Minto Circle in 1875. It was a boarding school attached to his Aligarh

Muslim University, which sat 130 kilometres from Delhi along the Delhi–Calcutta Grand Trunk Road.

It was the scorching heat of the North Indian plains that first made me think, 'I am not home.' It is a cruel thing to ask a valley dweller to live in a tropical, dry climate zone and withstand a minimum summer temperature of a hundred degrees Fahrenheit. It was, initially, the most difficult thing the eight of us had to face at boarding school.

Often, at night, we would leave our rooms, gather on the lawn and talk about home: our home of forests, where rivulets and streams criss-cross spring valleys, where the mighty Himalayas wear blankets of snow till late summer and the cooling scent of pine cones fills the air. The great Mughal emperor Jehangir had rightly called it 'paradise on earth'. All this contrasted sharply with our new surroundings in Aligarh, and we always looked for an excuse to travel home.

The morning newspapers of 6 December 1992 brought the news that 150,000 Kar Sevaks (Hindu nationalist volunteers) were heading to Babri Masjid in Ayodhya to claim the disputed land. Large contingents of police and paramilitaries had been deployed to stop the Kar Sevaks from entering Ayodhya.

Babri Masjid was a mosque built in 1527 by Babur, the founder of the Mughal empire that ruled India for more than two centuries. For many years, India had witnessed alarming politicking on the issue. The Hindu right, including the mainstream Bharatiya Janata Party, argued that the mosque was previously called Masjid-i-Janmasthan (Mosque of the Birthplace), acknowledging the site as the birthplace of the Hindu deity Lord Rama. This, they concluded, meant that they should be allowed to demolish the mosque and build a Hindu temple on the site.

On the afternoon of 6 December, we were having lunch when we heard that the Kar Sevaks had broken through the security cordon and entered the mosque complex. An uneasy silence descended on our dorm. A few hours later, the news came that the Kar Sevaks had climbed over the three mighty domes of the mosque and razed it to the ground.

As soon as the news broke, more than 25,000 students from Aligarh Muslim University (AMU) piled out onto Anoopshahra Road in protest, burning a dozen vehicles. It was late into the night before the authorities were able to gain control over the rioting students.

Early the following morning, a curfew was imposed in Aligarh and other cities in Uttar Pradesh, and in Delhi and Mumbai. In the ensuing Hindu–Muslim riots more than 2,500 people were reportedly killed. Soon after the riots, an indefinite curfew was imposed in Aligarh city and the Civil Lines area adjacent to the university campus.

In the evening, one of my Kashmiri friends, Farhat, knocked frantically on my door to tell me that the curfew was likely to continue for many days and that the authorities were trying to close the campus indefinitely. They were arranging special buses for the students; these would be escorted out by security staff and would drop the students at the railway station, where they could take trains home. Farhat told me that if I wanted to go I would have to be at the proctor's office tomorrow morning before the bus left for the railway station. He then rushed on to tell Assif Bodha, another Kashmiri student at Minto Circle.

The riots had prevented the school's food suppliers from making their usual delivery. That night, I slept with my stomach half full and felt the pain of not having eaten enough. I could not resist indulging in a powerful nostalgia for delicious, home-made *waẓwan*, a multi-course, meat-based Kashmiri feast.

The next morning, after a breakfast of tea and stale bread in the dining hall, I went straight to Farhat's room and told him that I was also going. I hurried to my room and started packing my belongings into a suitcase. The year before, I had taken my ninth-grade books home after finishing the annual exam. My mother, who is a teacher and fond of Islamic literature, had been thrilled to read my ninth-grade theology textbook – an Urdu book of Islamic anecdotes. She had told me to bring her my tenth-grade theology textbook when I came home for the winter vacation.

I threw the book into my suitcase along with a few T-shirts and my jeans and ran to Farhat's room. Farhat – a short, stout boy who spent most of his time in the reading room – was brimming with excitement at the thought of going home. We headed to the proctor's office to catch the bus and were glad to see all of our Kashmiri friends waiting.

About fifty metres from the school, the bus left the narrow university road to join the main Aligarh–Anoopshahra road. We were overwhelmed by the massive devastation and desolation on both sides of it: buses, set on fire by the rioters, had been reduced to iron skeletons; debris from destroyed *dhabas*, roadside restaurants, was scattered all over. Police trucks full of soldiers in riot gear were lined up near Tasveer Mahal, a cheap cinema hall where students from AMU and rickshaw-pullers went to watch movies.

We got to the railway station around two o'clock. There was a long queue. Aligarh's railway station had recently been compu-terized, and the operator was struggling with the keyboard of his brand-new computer; the monitor was still wrapped in a transparent polythene cover. As people talked and jeered at the ticket operator, there was an announcement: 'Attention, passengers! Fayazabad Special 31223 from Fayazabad to New Delhi is arriving on Platform 3. All passengers travelling to Delhi are requested to come to Platform Number 3. Indian Railway wishes you a happy and comfortable journey.'

We were so immersed in the joy of homecoming that none of us noted that this was not a routine train, but a special coming from Fayazabad, where the Kar Sevaks had wreaked havoc just a day before.

We hurried to Platform 3. After waiting a minute, we heard the discordant horn of the train. There were not many passengers on the platform. The riots had created a sense of panic that had affected life at railway stations as well. The porter with his red apron was missing; so, too, were the tea stall and the magazine and newspaper sellers.

Amid the engine's roar, I boarded the train, with Farhat and Javid Indrabi following me. Javid was an undergraduate student at Aligarh Muslim University and was travelling home to Ratnipora village in South Kashmir.

The rest of my fellow Kashmiri students entered the same coach from the rear door. Once I was inside, I started walking toward them, past the half-asleep passengers. The coach was jam-packed, and after passing four or five full berths, I gave up hope of getting a seat, lowered my suitcase and placed it between my legs. I stood still for a while in the aisle and noticed Farhat and Javid a few berths behind me. Farhat, chewing on bubble-gum, beamed at me. Javid was just behind him. He wore a blue pullover with white stripes running from collar to cuffs, and was listening to his Walkman.

My eyes moved to the berths on the other side of the corridor. There were about ten people facing one another in the lower berths of the compartment. Some of them were playing cards, others keenly watching, and almost half of them were smoking *biris*. A man wearing a white vest and a *dhoti* and holding a few cards in his left hand and a *biri* in his right, looked at me and said, *'Baya agay challo agay!'* (Brother, move ahead!)

I replied, *'Agay kanha, agay koi jaga Nahi ha.'* (There is no room ahead.)

The man paused. He stared at me and then shouted, *'Arrey ye tou Kashmiri lagta ha!'* (Hey, he looks Kashmiri!) Before I could utter another word, he went on, *'Maroo!'* (Beat him to death!)

Moments later, the people on the upper berths had come down and pounced on me, some of them slapping, some kicking. A huge, bulky man held me from behind and pointed a knife at my throat. Before he could cut my throat, I started shouting, 'I am a Kashmir Pandit! Please don't kill me! My uncle was killed by terrorists in Kashmir. Our houses have been burned by Muslims in Kashmir. We have been thrown out of the valley. I was living in a migrant camp at Jammu.'

They stopped, and one of them, who appeared to be the gang leader, kicked one of his co-passengers from his seat and ordered me to sit down.

'What is your name?'

'Hilal Bhatt.' I put the stress on the end of Bhatt, attempting to give it a Hinduized pronunciation.

'What is your father's name?' he said.

'Badri Bhatt,' I replied. I knew a few Hindu names from my Pandit friends, teachers, and neighbours in Kashmir. Badri was one whose first syllable aligned with my father's real name, Bashir.

There were no more questions. After taking the corner seat of a berth, I noticed a dozen worn bricks beneath the opposite

seat. Following my gaze, a fellow passenger told me these were
bricks from the demolished Babri Masjid, proof of their victory,
to be displayed proudly in their villages. I realized that these
were the Kar Sevaks, returning from Ayodhya.

My memory of what happened next is a bit like a fast-
moving action shot on a TV screen that suddenly goes blank
in a power cut.

The Kar Sevaks attacked Farhat and Javid, who had not
faked their identity as I had. What I recall is Farhat hiding
his face with both hands. As soon as he did, someone forced a
trident (an emblem of the god Shiva, carried by many of the Kar
Sevaks) into his chest, provoking a piercing cry, '*Hatai mojai!*'
(Oh, Mother!).

A shabbily dressed man stabbed a knife into his neck and a
fountain of blood arose from my friend's throat. Then the TV
power-cut moment: everything went blank.

That was the last I saw of my friend. I did not see what
happened to Javid, who was attacked several berths away, out
of my view. It was not until a month later that Javid's family
were able to trace his grave to a small village in Bulland Shahar
town. A local imam had arranged for his burial. Farhat's dead
body reached home three days later.

After five or ten minutes, the gang leader returned, his white
vest covered in blood. I overheard him saying, 'I've cut them
into pieces and thrown them away.' He removed his blood-
soaked vest and threw it out the window.

Turning to me, he told me he was glad I had revealed my
identity in time and promised to visit me in Jammu during
his next visit to Vaishnav Devi – the famous Hindu temple
in the hillocks of Jammu that thousands of pilgrims visit
every year.

The train continued toward Delhi. Somewhere close to Khurjah, a group of infuriated Muslims had assembled near the railway track with a supply of stones. As the 'Fayazabad Special' passed by, they pelted it with the stones. The Kar Sevaks pulled the iron shutters down over the windows, darkening the already suffocating atmosphere in the coach.

Minutes later, somebody announced that there were more Kashmiris in the coach. A few of the Kar Sevaks, bearing tridents, knives, and swords, went to see, and within seconds all the rest of my Kashmiri friends had been rounded up. The berth that I had been sitting on was cleared, and they were told to sit.

The Kar Sevaks started gathering everybody's bags and suitcases to be searched for valuables. I trembled with fear when I recalled the Urdu theology textbook that I had brought for my mother. I rose from my seat, picked up my suitcase and tried to put it amongst the checked luggage. The gang leader grabbed the suitcase and asked me what I was doing. I nervously replied that it was mine and that I wouldn't mind if he wanted to check it.

'No, it's all right if it's yours. You are our brother. In fact, you should help us to search these bags.'

Rafiq Ahmad, a postgraduate in fisheries, was the eldest of us Kashmiri students on the 'Fayazabad Special'. He asked to go to the toilet but was not allowed. He threatened that he would have no choice but to urinate on the seat.

The gang leader asked two of his boys to escort him to the toilet. Rafiq went inside the toilet and bolted the iron door. A few minutes later when the Kar Sevaks knocked at the door, he did not reply. They started kicking the door but still Rafiq did not open it. 'When you come out, we will cut you into pieces,' his escort threatened, but after a while they returned to their seats.

The train slowly pulled into Khurjah railway station. When it stopped at the station, Rafiq quietly opened the toilet door and jumped out of the train.

I looked out the window and saw Rafiq running across the train track. The Kar Sevaks, armed with knives, followed him, shouting, 'Kashmiri *dahshatgarud*' (Kashmiri terrorist).

Before he could jump onto the platform, a Kar Sevak grabbed him and stabbed him in the head. The train blew the horn and started pulling out of the station. The Kar Sevaks rushed back, leaving Rafiq lying in a pool of blood on the railway track.

We were still an hour away from Delhi. There was no certainty that they wouldn't pull down my trousers and check whether I was a Muslim that way. I had successfully managed to hide my identity, but what about physical verification? What if someone started questioning me – why, as a Hindu, had I preferred to study at a Muslim University? What if somebody opened my suitcase and found the theology textbook?

I decided I would try to get off the train at the earliest opportunity.

After their luggage had been thoroughly searched, all the remaining Kashmiri students were asked to line up. They were then were thrown out of the moving train. It was sheer luck that none of them was killed.

As the train approached the next stop, Ghaziabad station, I decided to get off. I politely told the Kar Sevaks that one of my uncles was living there and I was visiting him before going home. I gave them my fake Jammu address and started moving toward the back door of the coach. The train slowed down. I stood at the door and waited for the train to reach the platform and stop, and somebody behind me kicked me so hard that I fell out of the train.

Ignoring my injuries, I got up, looked toward the platform and spotted a person dressed in khaki about three hundred meters away. I ran toward him, crying, 'Help me, please, they will kill me! Help me please, they will kill me!'

'Who will kill you?' the man asked.

I looked back and there was no one there. I had assumed that they were following me with their knives in their hands. I told the man, who I now saw was a railway sweeper, what had happened to Farhat, Javid and Rafiq.

'You should talk to the police. There's a police station on Platform 1,' he said.

I walked up to the platform. By the time I got there the 'Fayazabad Special' had already left and there was a local train standing on the track. I noticed a signboard that said 'Police.' I opened the door and went inside. There was a middle-aged policeman sitting on a chair, looking at some papers, and I told him what had happened.

'You just wait. I will call our Sahib,' he said.

I waited, and as I looked around the room, I noticed the large, framed picture of Lord Rama hanging on a wall. It was decorated with flower garlands, and the remains of several incense holders were pinned to the bottom of the frame, their ashes scattered on an uncovered cement surface just below.

I decided, on impulse, that I should run away from the police office. I sneaked out the door and stopped at an empty coach of the local train to New Delhi. I stepped in and noticed somebody sitting in the corner. His head was covered with a cloth and his hands were holding his bag tightly. I stepped closer and was startled by a muffled yelp: 'Hilal!'

Assif, a Minto Circle classmate, had survived after the Kar Sevaks had thrown him from the train. His right arm was broken and blood oozed from his wounded head. Assif had taken a pair of trousers from his bag and tied it around his head to stop the blood.

The local train pulled away, and Assif changed his clothes, dumping his blood-soaked shirt and trousers in his bag. For the next hour we did not speak a word. Nor did I mention Farhat, Javid or Rafiq.

At New Delhi railway station, the Shalimar Express to Jammu was waiting for its passengers. We scanned each coach, looking for people with turbans and long beards. We found one, and passed the rest of the journey safely, in the company of Sikhs.

Angana P. Chatterji

The Militarized Zone

India asks us, 'Why do you throw stones?' No one asks, 'Who burned your house down?'

> Kashmiri youth, tortured in detention[1]

Srinagar, 9 January 2011.[2] Amid the disquiet of winter, I listen to torture survivors recounting their life stories. 'I am neither a stone-pelter nor a politician. I protest unfreedom,' Bebaak tells me.[3] Now nineteen years old, he participated in street protests in the summers of 2009 and 2010. 'The police said I would be arrested unless I stopped going to rallies. Then the police filed a First Information Report against me because I protest. What are the charges? That I refused subjugation?'

In 2010, Bebaak was detained for more than ten days, in violation of habeas corpus. While in custody, he was tortured: struck repeatedly and violently and denied medical treatment. Other youths in custody at that time were water-boarded. Some were forced to remove their clothes, then threatened with sodomy. Officials

---

1 Personal communication, January 2011. Name withheld for reasons of security.
2 Srinayar is the summer capital of the state of Jammu and Kashmir.
3 *Bebaak*: The word means 'Outspoken' in Urdu. Real name withheld for reasons of security, and certain information omitted or left vague.

attempted to coerce Bebaak into admitting that he had thrown stones and destroyed police property. Refusing to admit to crimes he had not committed, Bebaak was locked up in isolation, where he was beaten again. He recounts how, taking turns, two officers held him down while a third struck him with a baton, the butt of a rifle, and an iron chain: 'They only stopped when they were tired.'

Bebaak and other youths I speak with testify that the physical attacks were accompanied by verbal abuse: 'Your "race" is deranged. You are criminals. You are thieves. Your mother is a whore. Your sister will be raped by your people who are crazed. You will never see *azadi.*'

'In the jail, in the dark, as I lose consciousness', Bebaak says, 'I think, "We Kashmiris are a people, not a race. Our struggles against India's brutalities do not make us criminals." '

Bebaak's father was taken into custody when he inquired about his son. In one incident, he was injured with a rod that delivered electric shocks. In another, he was asked to bring a bribe of fifty thousand Indian rupees for Bebaak's release. 'When one member of the family participates in protest movements, they [Indian forces] try to break the spirit of the family,' Bebaak says. 'They try to destroy the economy of the neighbourhood in which we live, to turn our people against us. They say that if we want to stop the violence, we have only to stop our protest.'

State violence and abuse have left their imprint on Bebaak's body; he lives with physical and psychological trauma. Many are fearful to speak out against their repression, but Bebaak is defiant, resilient. 'I support *azadi,*' he says. 'How is it wrong to resist one's bondage?'

I have travelled to Kashmir as co-convener of the International People's Tribunal on Human Rights and Justice in India-

administered Kashmir. Outside the hotel where I am staying, intelligence personnel and sometimes men with guns are
stationed to keep watch over me at the behest of Indian state
agencies. Visitors are monitored, and many are stopped and
questioned before being allowed inside the hotel. Whether I
travel within Srinagar or outside, cars follow me. Phone calls
are tapped. All in order to pry, intimidate, restrict movement
and thought.

Each dimension of life in India-governed Kashmir is replete
with the obsessions and absurdities of militarization. Every
street, neighbourhood, public building and private establishment, forest and field, and road and alleyway has been 'secu-
ritized'. The overwhelming presence of the military, paramilitary, and police, of their guns and vehicles, of espionage
cameras, interrogation and detention centres, of army canton-
ments and torture cells, orders civilian life. Kashmir is a land-
scape of internment, where resistance is deemed 'insurgent' by
state institutions.

Later that day, after speaking with Bebaak, I meet Khurram
Parvez at our office at Lal Chowk. Khurram is a human rights
defender, an amputee who lives with the daily targeting that
ethical dissent begets.[4] 'We make choices in living in Kashmir,'
he says. 'To be silent when people are being brutalized is refusing to take responsibility. It is our moral obligation to take

---

4   Parvez is part of the International People's Tribunal on Human Rights
and Justice in India-administered Kashmir. His leg was severed by a land-
mine in 2004, while he was on a trip to monitor an election. This mine had
been placed by militants. In 2009, Parvez participated in a campaign to secure
a commitment from militants to abandon the use of mines. The Government
of India is not a signatory to the Convention on the Prohibition of the Use,
Stockpiling, Production and Transfer of Anti-Personnel Mines and on their
Destruction.

responsibility, to resist in principled ways.' Responsibility requires we bear witness as a call to action.

The word *freedom* represents many things across India-ruled Kashmir. But these divergent interpretations are steadfastly united on one point: freedom always signifies an end to India's illiberal governance.

In the administration of brutality, India, the former colony, has proven itself equal to its former colonial masters. Governing Kashmir is about India's coming of age as a power. Kashmir is the result of a fixation with haphazard and colonially imposed borders.[5] India overwrites memory – histories of violence, conflict, partition, and events that remain unresolved – to maintain the myth of its triumphant unification as a nation-state with Kashmir at its headspring. India's control of Kashmir requires that Kashmiri demands for justice be depicted as a threat to India's integrity.

Marshalling colonial legacies, the post-colonial state seeks to consolidate the nation as a new form of empire, demanding hyper-masculine militarization and territorial and extra-territorial control. This requires the manufacture of internal and external enemies to constitute a national identity, constructed in opposition to the anti-national and non-native enemies of the nation.

Hindu majoritarianism – the cultural nationalism and political assertion of the Hindu majority – anctifies India as

---

5 Unless otherwise specified, 'Kashmir' refers to India-held Kashmir. India governs the largest fragment of Jammu and Kashmir, including the Kashmir Valley, Jammu, Ladakh, and a major portion of the Siachen glacier. Pakistan controls Azad Kashmir and northern areas of Gilgit and Baltistan. China controls Aksai Chin and the Shaksgam Valley.

intrinsically Hindu and marks the non-Hindu as its adversary.[6] Hindu majoritarian culture has been consolidating its power despite the interventions of secular, syncretic, and progressive stakeholders. *Race* and *nation* are made synonymous in India, as Hindus – the formerly colonized, now governing, elite – are depicted as the national race.[7]

India's contrived enemy in Kashmir is a plausible one: the Muslim 'Other', the historically manufactured nemesis of Hindu-dominant India. India's political and media establishments caricature the Kashmiri Muslim as violent, impure, anti-national, as one who does not belong and who has refused political, cultural, and economic assimilation. The Kashmiri, historically residing outside the present Indian nation, is branded 'seditious' for seeking a different self-determination, for not belonging, and for not accepting annexation.

Amid the unresolved histories of the subcontinent, the resistance in disputed Jammu and Kashmir has been ongoing since 1931, when it was signalled by the 13 July uprising and the establishment of the All India Kashmir Committee.[8] The conflict morphed in October 1947, with the increasing encroachment

---

6   Some Hindus (Brahmins, northern Indians) are deemed more 'authentic' than others, and their special privileges are institutionalized. Epic violence has been perpetrated by Hindu nationalists in recent times, against Muslims in Gujarat (2002) and Christians in Orissa (2007, 2008).

7   Influenced by Nazi Germany and Fascist Italy, and the construction of the Jew as the internal enemy in the West, Savarkar, a Hindu nationalist leader, stated in 1923: '*Hindutva [Hinduness/Hindu supremacism] is not a word but a history . . . not only a Nation but also a race*'. See V. D. Savarkar, *Hindutva*, New Delhi: Hindi Sahitya Sadan, 2003, pp. 84–85.

8   The All India Kashmir Committee was established to secure the rights and freedoms of Muslims in Kashmir.

of repressive Indian sovereignty.[9] The period between 1947 and 1987 witnessed locally motivated, non-violent struggles for popular sovereignty and political self-determination.[10] In the post–Cold War era, the Kashmir conflict has been framed by discourses on 'terror politics'. The armed resistance in Kashmir began in 1988 and intensified following the Gawakadal killings in Srinagar in January 1990. The armed struggle abated between 2004 and 2007, yielding to a new phase of non-violent resistance.

The Indian state, however, propagates the misleading idea that the resistance movement is not locally inspired, that it aspires to violent resolutions, and that such aspirations are subsidized by Pakistan. These misconceptions ignore the fact that although Kashmiris did travel to Pakistan to seek arms training, such activity was largely confined to the early days of the armed resistance, the late 1980s through the mid-1990s. Today, the crisis of state in Pakistan, and the role of its ruling elite in vitiating people's democratic processes, does remain a pitfall for regional security. Pakistan's Directorate for Inter-Services Intelligence (ISI), responsible for domestic and foreign intelligence, with its perilous links with terror groups such as the Taliban, continues to infiltrate borders and endanger the region.

State racism – the primacy of Hindu majoritarian will in

---

9   Three wars have been fought over Kashmir, in 1947-8, 1965, and 1971 between India and Pakistan, and one in Kargil in 1999.

10   The argument for self-determination was recognized in the United Nations Resolutions of 1948; the promise of a plebiscite was made by India's first prime minister, Jawaharlal Nehru (to rethink the temporary accession of Jammu and Kashmir to India by the Hindu-descended maharaja, Hari Singh); and Article 370 of the Indian Constitution gives Kashmir the right to live under its own laws.

state decisions – orders India's rule in Kashmir.[11] India's rule in Kashmir merges neoliberal democracy with authoritarian practices. The Government of Jammu and Kashmir and the Indian Armed Forces neutralize the independent functioning of the judiciary, educational institutions, and the media in the name of national security, continuing what is in effect military governance.

India, the post-colony, silences revolt. In Kashmir, violence is part of the fabric of everyday life. India's governance of Kashmir requires the use of disciplinary practices and massacre as techniques of social control. Discipline is used on individuals and collectives by those authorized to perpetrate violence in the interest of the 'national good': the police, intelligence agencies, and paramilitary and armed forces. Discipline is effected through surveillance and punishment, in order to exact fear and obedience. Discipline flows through the formal and extra-legal capillaries of the state. Death is disbursed both through 'extrajudicial' means and those authorized by law. Discipline rewards forgetting, isolation, and depoliticization.

Summer 2010 saw a new phase in India's manoeuvring against Kashmir's determination to decide its own future. Amid the civil society's indefatigable uprisings in favour of *azadi* in this third summer since 2008, the recurring use of violence by the Indian forces has been deliberate; their tactics have been cruel and precise.[12]

---

11   Racisms of state. See M. Foucault, *Society Must Be Defended, Lectures at the Collège de France, 1975-1976*, trans. D. Macey, New York: Picador, 2003.
12   This section is based on research which I undertook between June and November 2010, with follow-up in March 2011.

Summer 2010 witnessed strikes and mass protests, as hundreds and thousands of people marched through the streets, in cities, towns, and rural areas across Kashmir to protest against the suppression of civil society. Graffiti, songs, comic strips, prose and poetry were all used as mediums of dissent. Crowds carried banners demanding 'Go, India, Go Back'; they daubed 'Indian Dogs Go Home' on the pavements; the call for India to 'Quit Kashmir' rent the air. It was reminiscent of another epoch in history, the 'Quit India' movement of 1942, against British colonial rule.

Dominant Indian representations of the situation described the mass civil disobedience as something engineered by pro-freedom groups or cross-border interests, rather than a spontaneous response by the people to their experience of subjugation. Armed forces personnel characterized it not as civil disobedience but as 'agitational terrorism', and criminalized Internet-based protest, terming it 'cyber terrorism'.

Between 11 June and 22 September 2010, India's police, paramilitary, and military killed 109 Kashmiri youths, men, and women. Indian forces opened fire on crowds, tortured children, detained elderly people without explanation, and coerced false confessions. There were seventy-three days of curfew and seventy-five days of strikes and agitation. On 11 September, the day of Eid-ul-Fitr, celebrating the end of Ramadan, the assault continued. Large demonstrations, identified as a threat rather than an expression of rightful civil disobedience, were targeted by the Indian forces. The paramilitary and police verbally abused and physically attacked civilian dissenters. The Indian forces acted with the knowledge and sanction of the Government of India and the Government of Jammu and Kashmir.

Summer 2010 was not unprecedented. It was not the first

time that the use of public and summary execution and civic torture had been considered necessary to subjugate Kashmir. The violence was a ritualistic reassertion of India's power over Kashmir's body.

Relentless state violence and the criminalization of non-violent means of self-expression led Kashmiris to resort to stone-throwing. Continued repression prompted the civil society to engage in acts of violence and arson in some instances. Each instance of civilian violence was fomented by the Indian forces' indiscriminate and pre-emptive use of force on civilians, force that included extrajudicial killings. The effect was cumulative. In peaceable civilian demonstrations, women and men protested the actions of Indian forces. Individuals caught in the midst of the unrest, or gathering to mourn the death of a civilian protester, were fired upon by state security, leading to more protests and to the ever greater use of force by the police and paramilitary: torture, killings, vandalizing of neighbourhoods. In response to that came larger, and sometimes violent, civilian protests, which in turn precipitated further state repression.

Paramilitary and police killings were not limited to encounters with protesters. On 12 June, *Muhammad Rafiq Bangroo*, twenty-four years old, was standing near his home watching the protests when he was set upon and severely beaten by the paramilitary Central Reserve Police Force (CRPF). He died a week later at the Sher-e-Kashmir Institute of Medical Sciences Hospital in Srinagar. *Yasmeen Jan*, age twenty-five, from the Srinagar town of Dander Khah, was killed by a bullet fired into her chest by CRPF and/or police personnel on 6 July, while she stood near a window inside her home.

On 19 July, CRPF and police personnel fired at a peaceful funeral procession carrying the body of *Faizan Bhuroo*. Faizan, a minor, drowned on 17 July after he jumped into the Jhelum River when Special Operations Group personnel attempted to arrest him as he returned home from the Main Chowk in Baramulla district. Faizan's funeral procession was intercepted while on its way to the district commissioner's office to lodge a protest. The procession was attacked without provocation; in the clashes that followed, a large gathering of protesters threw stones. Police opened fire, killing *Faya\z Ahmad Khanday*, twenty-three years old. The crowd, infuriated, escalated to acts of arson, including an attempted attack on the house of a police officer allegedly involved in the drowning of Faizan Bhuroo.

Sameer Ahmad Rah, nine years old, died from the beatings he received from CRPF personnel on 2 August. Found playing near where a demonstration had taken place earlier in the day, he was grabbed, mutilated and killed by CRPF personnel. The torture they inflicted on him included driving a bamboo stick into his mouth.

In India, politicians and the media blamed protesters for the remorseless violence of the state. But civil society demonstrations in Kashmir are not, as has been reported, a law-and-order problem. Stone-throwing and acts of arson are not the causes of the violence that is endemic in Kashmir today. Nobody has been killed by protesters throwing stones.[13] Pro-freedom leaders (the Indian state uses the reductive term 'separatists') have emphasized non-violent civil disobedience and have exhorted people not to react violently to the violence and killings by Indian forces.

---

13   A case alleging that stone-throwing led to the death of Shafiq Ahmad Sheikh was registered in April 2010. Investigations conducted by journalists uncovered information that Sheikh's murder and the registration of the case were linked to subterfuge.

Distinctions in method and power – dissimilarities between the strategies of the Indian state and those of Kashmiri dissenters, between stone pelters and armed soldiers, between 'terrorists' (as Kashmiri dissenters are branded by the state) and 'freedom fighters' (as Kashmiri protesters designate themselves) – are ignored. In summer 2010, India's prime minister, Manmohan Singh, focused on the need for efficient tactics in 'crowd control'. India's intelligentsia, inured to the idea of 'rational' state violence, assessed the costs and benefits of military action. State violence is accepted as the sine qua non for the maintenance of the Indian nation.

The Government of India continues to monitor the resistance movement, shifting the definition of what does or does not constitute an acceptable exercise of civil liberties. Kashmiris are allowed to protest in New Delhi, but in Kashmir, sloganeering is met with force. When in July 2010 Masarat Alam Bhat, a rising pro-freedom leader, issued a written appeal to Indian soldiers to 'Quit Kashmir', Indian authorities banned its circulation.

As state-sponsored aggression increased, protestors were provoked into further acts of violence. On 13 September 2010, crowds protesting Florida pastor Terry Jones's call to desecrate the Quran torched a Christian missionary school and some government offices. On that day alone, eighteen civilians were killed by Indian forces across Kashmir; a police officer also died. Provoking Kashmiri dissenters to violence served to confirm the dominant story of Muslims as 'violent', even though several pro-freedom leaders condemned the attack on the Christian school and renewed their call for non-violent dissent.

On 25 September, while the 65th Session of the United Nations General Assembly met in New York City, New Delhi announced an eight-point plan, the object of which was to maintain the status quo in Kashmir while keeping the disorder and violence there concealed from the international gaze. The plan committed India to releasing youths who had been arrested and detained without trial during the protests that summer; that commitment was never acted upon. The plan also proposed setting up task forces in Jammu and Ladakh to monitor and assess the situation in Kashmir. However, no task force was proposed for assessing the impact of India's governance on Kashmir. Neither did the plan propose any reduction in troops.

The plan did promise compensation payments of 500,000 rupees (rather than the customary 100,000 rupees) to the next of kin of victims killed by Indian forces. However, it made no commitment to investigate the killings of more than a hundred Kashmiris by the Indian forces that summer. ' "Shining India" can afford to pay a larger price for murdering Kashmiris,' one Kashmiri youth noted derisively. 'Is the plan to continue to kill us, just for a better price?'[14]

The plan proposed one billion Indian rupees to rebuild Kashmir's educational infrastructure. What is the status of academic freedom in Kashmir? Students in the arts, humanities, and the social sciences who seek to study the conflict and issues of violence and militarization are rarely permitted to do so. Kashmiri students who are related to former or deceased militants have not been permitted to travel abroad even when they have secured scholarships to do so.

The plan stated that New Delhi would support the efforts of the Government of Jammu and Kashmir to review and repeal detention cases filed under the Public Safety Act (PSA) of 1978. No action has

---

14   Personal communication, via telephone, September 2010. Name withheld for reasons of security.

ensued. The PSA is a preventive-detention law that, among other provisions, authorizes incarceration for up to two years on grounds of unconfirmed suspicion. In March 2011, Amnesty International reported that between eight thousand and twenty thousand people have been held under the PSA over the past twenty years.[15]

On 13 September 2010, the Government of India stated its willingness to engage with Kashmiri groups that reject violence. New Delhi did not apply the same precondition of non-violence to itself. Nor did it acknowledge that pro-freedom groups have repeatedly opposed the use of violence in recent years. Misogynist and violent groups such as the Lashkar-i-Tayyaba (a Pakistani group), al-Qaeda, and the Taliban are mercenaries looking for takers in Kashmir. Per the Indian state's pronouncements, there are between only five hundred and a thousand militants in the Kashmir Valley today. These groups have been unsuccessful not because the Indian army is effective in controlling them but because Kashmiris have been uninterested in alliances with them.

If India fails to act, if Pakistan acts only in its own self-interest, and if the international community does not insist on an equitable resolution to the Kashmir dispute, it is conceivable that, forsaken by the world, Kashmiris will be prompted to take up arms again. If state repression persists, it is conceivable that the movement for non-violent dissent, mobilized since 2004, will erode. Signs indicate that it is already fraying. It is conceivable that India's brutality will induce Kashmiri youth to move from stones to petrol bombs, or worse.

If the mass movement in Kashmir descends into widespread

15 Amnesty International, 'A "Lawless Law": Detentions under the Jammu and Kashmir Public Safety Act', London: Amnesty International Limited, 2011.

violence, India will take advantage of the situation to reject Kashmiri demands for demilitarization and conflict resolution and to further entrench what is a civic and legal 'state of exception'. India will then reinforce further its armed presence in Kashmir, which is presently 671,000 strong.[16] If India succeeds in both provoking local armed struggle and in spreading the idea that Kashmiri resistance is linked to foreign terrorism from Pakistan and Afghanistan, rather than being the locally grown independence movement that it is, New Delhi will acquire international sanction to continue its Government of Kashmir on grounds of national security.

This policy of incitement is a mistake. Such legitimation of military rule will produce intractable conflict and violence. All indications are that in Kashmiri civil society dissent will not abate: it is not externally motivated but historically compelled. Repressive regimes tend to overlook that freedom struggles are not about the moralities of violence versus non-violence, but reflect a desire to be free. The oppressors forget that the greater the oppression, the more fervent the resistance. Violence is apt to reproduce itself in cycles.

Whether dissent in Kashmir continues as mass-based peaceful resistance or turns into organized armed struggle will depend upon India's political decisions. Any future mobilization by Kashmiris would involve an even stronger mass movement than that which occurred in 1990 and between 2004 and 2007, led by youth whose lives have been shaped by two decades of militarization. If this transpires, it may well be impossible to avoid the infiltration of violent groups into the Indian subcontinent

---

16   Figure is derived from government and journalistic sources, September 2011, and includes counter-terrorism and special forces.

– making such infiltration a self-fulfilling prophecy. Who wants that? Can South Asia, already nuclearized, survive that? The onus is on India to keep this from happening – not through the use of unmitigated force, but through listening to the demands for change made by Kashmiris.

I spent considerable time between July 2006 and January 2011 learning about and working in Kashmir, making sixteen separate trips to the region. In July 2006, the noted human rights lawyer Parvez Imroz invited me to collaborate in instituting the International People's Tribunal on Human Rights and Justice in India-administered Kashmir, which we convened on 5 April 2008, together with Zahir-Ud-Din, Gautam Navlakha, Mihir Desai, and Khurram Parvez.[17]

In undertaking work for the Tribunal, I have travelled through Kashmir's cities and countryside, from Srinagar to Kupwara, through Shopian and Islamabad/Anantnag.[18] I have witnessed the violence that India's military, paramilitary, and police perpetrate against Kashmiris. I have walked through the graveyards that hold Kashmir's dead, and have met with grieving families. I have listened to the testimony of a mother who sleepwalks to the grave of her son, attempting to resuscitate his body. I have met with the grave-diggers who were terrorized by Indian forces into performing the task of burial.

I recall Atta Mohammad's testimony from June 2008. In his seventies, he is the grave-digger and caretaker at Bimyar, where he buried 203 bodies between 2002 and 2006. He told me, 'My nights are tormented and I cannot sleep; the bodies and graves

17   See kashmirprocess.org for more on the Tribunal.
18   Both names have particular histories. Presently, in Kashmiri politicized discourse, local communities often identify Anantnag as Islamabad.

appear and reappear in my dreams. My heart is weak from this labour. I have tried to remember all this . . . the sound of the earth as I covered the graves . . . bodies and faces that were mutilated . . . mothers who would never find their sons. My memory is an obligation.'[19]

I have met with children and youth who were orphaned. I have met women whose sons were disappeared, and have witnessed the daily upheaval of anticipation and hopelessness in their lives. I have met with 'half-widows', women whose husbands have been 'disappeared'. Half-widows do not qualify for state support, such as the pensions offered to 'widows'. Women have been forced disproportionately to assume the task of caring for disintegrated families and to undertake the work of seeking justice following disappearances and deaths.

In June 2009, I travelled to Shopian to meet with the family of Asiya and Neelofar Jan, who were raped, reportedly by more than one perpetrator, then murdered. The complicity of Indian forces and state institutions pointed to obstruction of justice at the highest levels. The Shopian investigations, conducted by state institutions, shifted scrutiny from the paramilitary CRPF—recognized as an 'Indian' force—to the Kashmir police—understood as 'locals' (read: Muslims). The inquiry focused on manufacturing scapegoats to subdue public outcry—on 'control', rather than 'justice'.

In July 2010, I sat with witnesses and family members in Islamabad/Anantnag who described how Indian forces had

---

19   Taken from A. P. Chatterji, P. Imroz et al., *Buried Evidence: Unknown, Unmarked, and Mass Graves in Indian-Administered Kashmir, A Preliminary Report*, Srinagar: International People's Tribunal on Human Rights and Justice in Indian-administered Kashmir, 2009, 18.

chased down and executed three of their friends who had been involved in acts of civil disobedience. I spoke with human rights defenders and journalists who had been denied passports and the right to travel. I also spoke with people who had been targeted by militants in the 1990s but whose experience of the reprehensible atrocities of militancy had not diminished their desire for self-determination, even as they do not have a realistic idea of what that should be.

I have met with torture survivors—non-militants and former militants alike—who testified to the sadism of Indian forces. Over 60,000 people have been tortured in interrogation centres: people who have been water-boarded, mutilated, and paraded naked, who have had petrol injected into their anuses, who have been raped, starved, humiliated, and psychologically tortured. An eagle tattoo on the arm of one man was reportedly identified by an army officer as a symbol of Pakistan-held Azad Kashmir. Though the man explained that the tattoo dated from his childhood, the tattooed skin was burned off. The man recalled the officer saying: 'When you look at this, think of *Azadi*.'

Indian forces stationed in schools and colleges verbally and physically harass girls. Many young women have been traumatized by the conduct of Indian soldiers, and at times have been compelled to use the *hijab* or *burkha* to create a barrier against the unwanted advances of the Indian forces. There are 671 security camps in Kashmir.[20] The structure and placement of the camps enforces contact between women, children, and Indian soldiers and creates contexts in which gender-based violence becomes endemic. Male youths and men refusing to participate

---

20   Figure derived from government and journalistic sources, October 2009.

in the sexual servitude of women have been sodomized. Third-gender and transgender youths have been threatened with rape.

Many have been forced to witness the rape of women and girl family members. A mother who was reportedly commanded to watch her daughter's rape by army personnel pleaded for her child's release. They refused. She then pleaded that she could not watch and asked to be sent out of the room or else killed. The soldier put a gun to her forehead, stating that he would grant her wish, and shot her dead before they proceeded to rape her daughter.

Since 1990, Kashmir's economy has incurred a loss of more than 1,880,000 million Indian rupees (US $40.4 billion). The collapse of the non-military political economy through the imposition of arbitrary borders and the impeding of livelihoods and trade has compounded class inequalities among disenfranchised, land-poor Kashmiri groups such as Gujjars, Bakarwals, and Hanjis. The refusal of land rights and land reforms has taken from labourers their means of subsistence.

In December 2009, the Tribunal released a report entitled *Buried Evidence*, which documents 2,700 hidden, unmarked, and mass graves, containing 2,943 bodies, mostly of men, across 55 villages in the Bandipora, Baramulla, and Kupwara districts of Kashmir. These bodies, bearing the marks of torture, burns, and desecration, were dragged through the night and buried next to homes, fields and schools. The graves were dug by locals on this village land at the behest of the military, paramilitary, and police.

The Indian forces claim that these graves house 'foreign militants'. In most cases, the bodies have not been exhumed and identified. When they have been, the dead were revealed to be local people, ordinary citizens, killed in 'fake encounters', that is, the extrajudicial killing of civilians in staged encounters with security forces. The Tribunal examined fifty alleged 'encounter' killings by Indian forces. In these cases, thirty-nine victims were of Muslim descent, four were of Hindu descent, and seven were of undetermined descent. Forty-nine of the fifty had been labelled militants or foreign insurgents by Indian forces. Forty-seven of them were found to have been killed in fake encounters. Only one person was identifiable as a local militant.

Who are the Indian forces? In Kashmir, Indian forces tend to be aligned with Hindu majoritarian interests but are drawn from disenfranchised castes and other outsider groups: Assamese, Nagas, Sikhs, Dalits – once known as Untouchables – even Muslims from Kashmir are being used to combat the Kashmiri population. The figures indicate the levels of tension: thirty-four soldiers committed suicide in Kashmir in 2008; fifty-two fratricidal killings took place between 21 January 2004 and 14 July 2009. Between January and early August 2010, sixteen soldiers committed suicide, and two died in fratricidal killings.

The laws authorize soldiers to question, raid houses, make arrests without bringing charges, intimidate, perpetrate custodial violence, and permit protracted detentions without due process. Citing 'national security', Indian forces in Kashmir shoot and kill on unverified suspicion, and are immune from prosecution.

All of these actions are deemed 'acts of service', and rewards and promotions are given to personnel for killing presumed insurgents.[21] This was exemplified in the Machil murders, which, it has been reported, were also motivated by the promise of cash rewards. On 30 April 2010, Indian Armed Forces claimed that

---

21　Human Rights Watch, *'Everyone Lives in Fear': Patterns of Impunity in Jammu and Kashmir*, New York: Human Rights Watch, 2006, 65–6.

three 'foreign/infiltrating militants' (from Pakistan) had been killed in an 'encounter' in the Machil sector of Kupwara district, along the Line of Control (LOC). The army reported that these killings had prevented armed combatants from crossing the LOC. On 28 May 2010, the three 'militants' were identified as Shahzad Ahmad, Riyaz Ahmad, and Mohammad Shafi, residents of Baramulla district in Indian-administered Kashmir, and their murders were authenticated as 'fake encounter' killings. The armed forces had been offering cash rewards of between 50,000 and 200,000 rupees to police or armed forces personnel for each militant killed. It has not been made public whether the relevant armed forces officers claimed 150,000 rupees in award monies for the three staged encounter killings in Machil.

Despite various debates since 2009, the Indian government has made no commitment to rescind the series of impunity laws deployed in the administration of Kashmir or to reverse the special powers, privileges, and immunity granted to the Indian forces there. Revoking the Armed Forces Special Powers Act alone will not stop the horror in Kashmir. India's laws are not the primary problem. Legal impunity is the cover for the moral impunity of Indian rule.

Neither has the Indian government shown any willingness to consider withdrawing military forces from Kashmir. Between 2002 and 2008, it procured US$5 billion dollars' worth of arms from the Israeli state to combat Islamic insurgents – a colossal sum for India,[22] where 38 per cent of the world's poor reside and where eight of the country's poorest states are more impoverished than the twenty-six poorest countries on the African

---

22   T. Ali, 'Not Crushed, Merely Ignored', *London Review of Books*, 22 July 2010.

continent. Five billion spent on arms, in addition to the other monies and resources invested in the militarization of Kashmir, does not imply an intent to withdraw.

India needs to make the 'Kashmir problem' disappear, to force Kashmiris to forsake their claim for independent statehood (or, for some, to be assimilated with Pakistan), or their demand for full autonomy. Military offensives and multi-track diplomacy seek to nullify civil society's legitimate anger and dissent. Diplomats and Indian peace agents traverse Kashmir, enacting the obligatory gestures of Track II Diplomacy, to secure a peace proposal that will be acceptable to India and, ostensibly, to Kashmiris.[23] Only very few of these initiatives are successful. The terms of reference set by New Delhi exclude discussions of self-determination or heightened autonomy, boundary negotiations, and the Siachen glacier and other critical water resources, as well as renegotiations over the route of the Line of Control.[24]

Kashmiris are fatigued by the interminable 'new beginnings' and the deadened political initiatives and confidence-building measures (CBMs) that accompany them. CBMs, which have tended to be about India–Pakistan relations, have not shifted the realities for Kashmiris. In April 2005, the bus service from Srinagar to Muzaffarabad was set up. There followed a number of other initiatives: an agreement, in October 2005, to establish a hotline between the maritime security agencies of India

---

23   Track II Diplomacy: Informal diplomacy, in which non-state actors engage in conflict resolution or confidence-building measures, often understood as a containment tactic.

24   The disputed 740-kilometre Line of Control (also cease-fire line, which includes the 550-kilometre Indian Kashmir border) established at the end of the First Kashmir War (1947–8) between India and Pakistan.

and Pakistan, allowing early exchange of information on fishing communities' infringement into each nation's territorial waters; a bus service from Lahore to Amritsar, started in January 2006; and, in May of the same year, an agreement to trade raw produce between the various regions of Jammu and Kashmir. This trade agreement did not take into account the needs of local communities and it has been ineffectual in energizing local economies.[25]

In August 2007, a prisoner exchange saw 72 Pakistani nationals released from India's gaols, with 135 Indian nationals going the other way. In April 2008, India signed a joint agreement with Afghanistan, Pakistan, and Turkmenistan for a $7.6 billion, 1,680-kilometre, environmentally controversial pipeline project expected to supply 3.2 billion cubic feet of natural gas by 2015. In May 2008, Junoon, the Pakistani rock band, gave an Indian government–sanctioned performance in Srinagar. In the same month, the foreign ministers of India and Pakistan proposed a series of Kashmir-focused CBMs, including a triple-entry permit to facilitate civilian movement across the Line of Control and permit consular outreach to prisoners.[26] No measures sought to reconnect communities and families whose ties were severed through Indo-Pak border politics.

In January 2009, for the eighteenth consecutive year, India and Pakistan exchanged lists of nuclear facilities located in their respective territories. Six months later, the prime ministers of India and Pakistan met on the sidelines of the Non-Aligned Movement summit in Egypt and issued a joint statement 'charting the way forward in India–Pakistan relations'.

---

25   This section is based on research I undertook between September and October 2010.
26   These were jettisoned following the terror attacks in Mumbai of 26–29 November 2008.

New Delhi and Islamabad appear to be in collusion. If Pakistan overlooks India's conflicts in Jammu and Kashmir, India seems willing to forget Pakistan's occupation of its own fragment, Azad Kashmir. And although Pakistan's politicians constantly flag India's injustices in 'Indian' Kashmir, they do not reciprocally address issues in the management of the Pakistan-held portion, including the undermining of movements for the unification of Kashmir. Access to Azad Kashmir remains restricted, and human rights violations there are not spoken of.[27] For Pakistan's government, Afghanistan is the current priority, not Kashmir. Kashmir's future as a democratic, inclusive, and pro-secular space is linked to what happens within India and Pakistan. Kashmir's resolution, however, cannot mean a sanction to Pakistan's encroachment on Afghanistan, which remains a highly likely possibility. For the United States and India, the containment of China is another issue, also linked to Kashmir. Conversations on the phased withdrawal of troops by India and Pakistan at the border, on local self-government or the creation of a joint supervision mechanism on Jammu and Kashmir, involving India, Pakistan, Indian Kashmir, and Pakistani Kashmir, are at an impasse.

India's actions are directed toward assuming a role as a world power, a world market, and a world negotiator in global politics. By pushing forward a diluted "autonomy," the Government in New Delhi is seeking to assimilate Kashmir irrevocably into the India nation-state. Local self-government – a weak autonomy – would be New Delhi's compromise, with a joint supervisory body made up of India, Kashmir, and possibly Pakistan.

---

27   Human Rights Watch, ' "With Friends Like These": Human Rights Violations in Azad Kashmir', New York: Human Rights Watch, vol. 18, no. 12(C), 2006.

What constitutes India's dialogue with Kashmiris in conditions of extreme subjugation? The Indian government's 'inclusive dialogue' in summer 2010 disregarded the demands of Kashmiri civil society. Conflict resolution and diplomatic processes are largely directed by the state, or by individuals and groups financed by it. New Delhi invited to the table various stakeholders from Kashmiri civil society, including rights groups and journalists. Bringing people to the table creates an image of inclusiveness, but there is no shift in the agenda. The Indian government's promises are empty and there has been no follow-through; such promises are a national public relations campaign for local and international consumption.

New Delhi also anticipates that the Kashmiri leadership, including pro-freedom groups, can be restrained and weakened by their own infighting. Indeed, certain sections of the pro-freedom religious and political leadership have shown themselves to lack vision, honesty, and the ability to prioritize collaboration for justice and peace in Kashmir; equally, elements of the leadership have been unable to collaborate meaningfully with civil society, or with observant Muslims, unobservant Muslims, and non-Muslims.

Mosques have functioned as spaces of refuge and forums for dissent, and were also used as granaries and shelters during the uprisings in 1931 and 1990, and in 2008 and 2009. Yet the theocratic elites have been unable to close the distance between themselves and the grassroots. The spiritual commitment to justice has diminished as religious politics have embraced realpolitik. The objective of freedom has been deferred in favour of smaller, more immediate political gains. This has enfeebled segments of the complex Hurriyat (Freedom) alliance, which has been unable to develop a framework for power sharing among constituents and is often unable to capitalize on the exuberant people's movement on the streets of Kashmir.[28]

Segments of the pro-freedom leadership and the Kashmiri elite have aligned with New Delhi rather than with Kashmiri civil society. New Delhi has encouraged this dynamic to create an elite collaborator class in Srinagar that undermines the will of the Kashmiri people. The complicity of Kashmir's collaborator class with India's state agenda reaps individual benefits, provides security for collaborators, and strengthens Indian national interest.

What do a majority of Kashmiris want? First, to secure a good-faith agreement with New Delhi and Islamabad on the right of Kashmiris to determine the course of their future, set a time-frame, and define the interim conditions necessary to proceed. Following this, civil society and political leaders must put in motion processes to educate, debate and consult with that society, including its minority groups, in sketching out the terms of reference for a resolution, prior to negotiations with India and Pakistan.

New Delhi is incredulous that Kashmiris overwhelmingly reject its overtures, criticizing Kashmiri youth for turning down the employment that India promises and for continuing to protest on the streets. The civil society's dissent is perhaps the solitary roadblock to New Delhi's course of intransigence against Kashmir's resolution. New Delhi has refused to acknowledge the extent of its human rights violations, and how integral they are to the maintenance of Indian control in Kashmir. New Delhi has not explained why militarization in Kashmir has been

---

28   The All Parties Hurriyat Conference, an alliance of over 20 groups and parties, including the Aawami Action Committee, Jammu and Kashmir Liberation Front, and People's Democratic Front.

disproportionately used to brutalize Kashmiris, when ostensibly the Indian forces are there only to secure the borderlands. Human rights violations cannot be stopped in Kashmir without removing the military. The military cannot be removed from Kashmir without rupturing India's will to power.

India also charges that in keeping alive the call to *azadi*, Kashmiri pro-freedom leaders prevent young people from attending schools and leading normal lives. 'Normality' is far outside the ambit of Kashmiris! India also disparages the Kashmiri pro-freedom leadership and speaks of the wealth and property these leaders have amassed. Scarce mention is made of leaders who are from working-class backgrounds. On the part played by the Indian state in corrupting political leaders in Kashmir, in order to distance the pro-freedom leadership from civil society, India is silent.

The Indian government's 'inclusive dialogue' fails to recognize Kashmir as an international dispute and conflict zone. Nor does it offer an immediate halt to, and moratorium on, extrajudicial killings by the Indian military, paramilitary, and police, or an immediate halt to, and moratorium on, the use of torture, kidnapping, enforced disappearance and gender-based violence by the Indian military, paramilitary, and police. Nor does it include a plan for the release of political prisoners, for the return of those exiled, or for resolving the issue of displacement; or agreements on an immediate 'soft border' policy between Kashmir, India and Pakistan to enable the resurgence of Kashmir's economy; or a commitment to the free exercise of civil liberties by Kashmiris, including the right to civil disobedience or freedom of speech, assembly, religion, movement and travel.

Neither does the 'inclusive dialogue' provide a plan for

proactive demilitarization and the immediate revocation of authoritarian laws. It fails to address the identification and dismantling of detention and torture centres, including those in army camps, and the return of 1,054,721 *kanals* of land occupied by Indian forces.[29] There is no mention of a plan for international and transparent investigations into the unmarked and mass graves created by the Indian military, paramilitary, and police. Or plans for a truth and justice commission, or political and psychosocial reparation and healing. Such omissions make a travesty of any process promising 'resolution' – they are a guarantee of continued disaffection on the streets of Kashmir.[30]

Hindu-majority cultural nationalism seeks to form the nation by cementing its territorial cohesion and geopolitical dominance. Kashmir is crucial to this recipe. New Delhi has been the self-appointed arbitrator in determining the justifications for Kashmir's claim to freedom. The Indian state is apprehensive that any change in the status quo in Kashmir would foster internal crises of gigantic proportions in India. Across the nation there is considerable discontent, as differences in culture, imagination, and aspiration are mortgaged to the idea of India as fabricated by its Hindu elite. Kashmir remains India's excuse to avoid dealing with its own internal matters. Adivasis (indigenous peoples), Dalits, disenfranchised caste groups, women, and religious, ethnic and gender minorities are tired of waiting for the continually deferred fulfilment of the nation's promises.

Forty-four million Adivasis have been displaced since 1947.

---

29   A *kanal* is equivalent to 510 square metres.
30   See www.kashmirprocess.org.

Central India has been torn asunder, and as Maoists are designated the latest 'national threat', national memory forgets the systematic brutalization of peoples in the tribal belt that led to the Maoist call to arms. Then there are the massacres of Muslims in Gujarat, riots against Christians in Orissa, suicides of desperate farmers, and the plight of peasants and Adivasis in the Narmada Valley, where dams are not the 'temples of modern India', but its burial grounds.

Indian civil society assumes that an autonomous or separate Kashmir would take the form of an Islamist state and would therefore be a threat to India's democracy. The assumption that a Muslim-majority state in Kashmir would be ruled by Islamist extremists in support of global terror reflects the racism of Hindu-dominated India. Indians of Hindu descent too easily overlook that India's own democracy is infused with Hindu cultural dominance. Indian civil society, in line with the inflamed Islamophobia that influences the polities of the West, assumes that Islam and democracy are incompatible. Indian society must rethink its characterization of Kashmiris as prevalently *Jamaati*—the Arabic word for 'assembly', but used by India to imply an Islamist or fundamentalist group.

The logic that predominantly Muslim Kashmir must either stay with secular India or join Muslim-dominated Pakistan is a function of India's and Pakistan's internal ideological needs and identity politics. Neither nation speaks to the foremost aspiration of Kashmiris. Neither acknowledges the histories of feudal and colonial betrayal, in which Kashmir's inclusion was sought in assembling India and Pakistan as nation-states. India all too easily forgets its own history under British rule, and the declaration of its freedom fighters that the oppressor does not have the privilege of judging when a people are 'deserving' of freedom.

Kashmir is a Muslim-majority space. The population of India-held Kashmir was recorded at approximately 6,900,000 people in 2008, and approximately 95 per cent of them are Muslim. Kashmir's future as a democratic, inclusive and pro-secular space is linked to what happens within India and Pakistan. Kashmiris who desire a different future must assess the difficult alliances yet to be built among Kashmir, Jammu (a Hindu nationalist stronghold), and Ladakh (with its Buddhist majority), and among Muslims and Hindu Pandits, Dogra Hindus, Buddhists, Sikhs, Christians, indigenous groups, and others.

Then there is the question of what lies ahead between Indian-held Kashmir and Pakistan-held Kashmir. Minority groups such as Kashmiri Pandits must resist the attempts of Hindu nationalists and state institutions to use the Pandit community to create opposition between Muslims and Hindus in Kashmir, a tactic intended to further religionize the issue and govern through communalization.

Where is the international community on the issue of Kashmir? In recent history, Palestine, Ireland, Tibet and Kashmir have shared common features. In Tibet, between 1949 and 1979, 1.2 million people died and 320,000 were made refugees. In Ireland from 1969 to 2010, 3,710 died. For Israel, the occupation of Palestine has resulted in 10,271 dead (1987–January 2011), with 4.8 million refugees registered with the United Nations (1947–June 2010). In Kashmir, 70,000 are dead and over 8,000 have been disappeared. More than 250,000 have been displaced (1989–2010), including minority Kashmiri Pandits of Hindu descent.[31] Between 209 and 765 Kashmiri Pandits have been killed.[32]

Confronting India's political and human rights violations in Kashmir has not been a priority for powerful nations, and the international human rights community has been reluctant to approach the issue of Kashmir and take meaningful action.

At a September 2010 meeting of the United Nations General Assembly, India focused on terrorism and national security and called for the expansion of the United Nations Security Council, with the objective of its own inclusion. India reiterated that Kashmir is 'an integral part of India' and identified the region as the 'target of Pakistan-sponsored militancy and terrorism'.

Unreflective support of India by the global North reduces state-sponsored injustice and violence in Kashmir to the status of collateral damage, justified as necessary to combat Pakistan-sponsored terrorism. This conflation of Kashmir with Pakistan stifles debate and condones atrocities. When British prime minister David Cameron visited India in July 2010, he was asked to refrain from bringing up the 'K word'. US president Barack Obama's visit to New Delhi in November 2010 was laden with prohibitions, the mention of India's rule in Kashmir and its larger human rights record among them. Right-wing Hindu advocacy groups have also been successful in securing the silence of many politicians on Capitol Hill on the issue of Kashmir. The

---

31 Human Rights Watch, 'India's Secret Army in Kashmir: New Patterns of Abuse Emerge in the Conflict', New York: Human Rights Watch, 1996; and M. Kolodner, 'Violence as Policy in the Occupations of Palestine, Kashmir, and Northern Ireland', Master's thesis, Amherst College, 1996.
32 M. Jaleel, '209 Kashmiri Pandits Killed Since 1989, Say J-K Cops in First Report', *Indian Express*, 4 May 2008.

Kashmiri diaspora, its exiled and new and old immigrant communities, remains ideologically and politically fragmented.

A culture of grief hangs like a shroud over Kashmir. The sounds of war haunt whole *mohallas* (neighbourhoods). Abandoned buildings and deserted public squares, bullet holes, bunkers and watchtowers, armed personnel and counter-insurgents mark Kashmiri lives.

In the course of our work, Parvez Imroz and I have been taken into custody and detained for questioning. An explosive device was thrown at Imroz's home in 2008, targeting his family. That year, a First Information Report charged Zahir-Ud-Din, editor of the *Etalaat* English daily, and me with acting to incite crimes against the state, following his publication of an article I wrote on mass graves. Khurram Parvez has been threatened, and he is constantly monitored. My mother, living alone in Kolkata, has been questioned by intelligence officers. I am stopped at immigration each time I enter or leave India.[33]

It is 1 November 2010, and my life partner, Richard Shapiro, a Jewish-American academic whose scholarly focus is not South Asia but Continental philosophy and anti-racist work, has been refused entry into India without reason or due process, presumably to target the Tribunal's work. I call Kashmir from Delhi International Airport, undecided whether I should stay or leave. Khurram Parvez tells me, 'Your coming here [Kashmir] today is necessary. If you do not come, this move to separate you from Richard will also become a move to further isolate Kashmiris.'[34] I

33 I am a citizen of India and a permanent resident of the United States.
34 Personal communication, November 2010. We share gratitude for the solidarity we have received from various international institutions and collectives, and from segments of Indian civil society, public officials, and the press.

proceed from the international terminal in Delhi to board the flight to Srinagar. The estrangements inflicted through nation-building on the subcontinent are palpable to me on this day, my own experience an eerie reminder of the state's reach into domestic life.

The conditions of everyday life in Kashmir reveal the web of violence in which its civil society is confined. Through summer heat and winter snow, across interminable stretches of concertina wire, broken window-panes, barricades, check-posts, and literal and figurative walls, the dust settles, only to rise again. The agony of loss. The desecration of life. Kashmir's spiritual fatalities are staggering. The dead are not forgotten; remembrance and mourning are habitual practices of dissent.

'We are not free. But we know freedom,' KP tells me. 'The movement is our freedom. Our dreams are our freedom. The Indian state cannot take that away. Our resistance will live.'[35]

---

35   Personal communication, September 2010.

Arundhati Roy

Seditious Nehru

Public statement, 27 October 2010

My reaction to today's court order directing the Delhi Police to file an FIR [First Information Report] against me for waging war against the state: Perhaps they should posthumously file a charge against Jawaharlal Nehru, too. Here's what he said about Kashmir:

27 October 1947

In a telegram to the prime minister of Pakistan, Liaquat Ali Khan, the Indian Prime Minister Pandit Jawaharlal Nehru said, 'I should like to make it clear that the question of aiding Kashmir in this emergency is not designed in any way to influence the state to accede to India. Our view, which we have repeatedly made public, is that the question of accession in any disputed territory or state must be decided in accordance with the wishes of the people, and we adhere to this view.' (Telegram No. 402, Primin-2227, dated 27 October 1947, to PM of Pakistan, repeating telegram addressed to PM of UK)

31 October 1947

In another telegram to the PM of Pakistan, Pandit Nehru said, 'Kashmir's accession to India was accepted by us at the request of the Maharaja's government and the most numerously representative popular organization in the state, which is predominantly Muslim. Even then it was accepted on condition that as soon as law and order had been restored, the people of Kashmir would decide the question of accession. It is open to them to accede to either Dominion then.' (Telegram No. 255, dated 31 October 1947)

2 November 1947

In his broadcast to the nation over All India Radio on 2 November 1947, Pandit Nehru said, 'We are anxious not to finalize anything in a moment of crisis and without the fullest opportunity to be given to the people of Kashmir to have their say. It is for them ultimately to decide. And let me make it clear that it has been our policy that where there is a dispute about the accession of a state to either Dominion, the accession must be made by the people of that state. It is in accordance with this policy that we have added a proviso to the Instrument of Accession of Kashmir.'

3 November 1947

In another broadcast to the nation, on 3 November 1947, Pandit Nehru said, 'We have declared that the fate of Kashmir is ultimately to be decided by the people. That pledge we have given not only to the people of Kashmir but to the world. We will not and cannot back out of it.'

21 November 1947

In his letter No. 368 Primin, dated 21 November 1947, addressed to the PM of Pakistan, Pandit Nehru said, 'I have repeatedly stated that as soon as peace and order have been established, Kashmir should decide on accession by plebiscite or referendum under international auspices such as those of United Nations'.

25 November 1947

In a statement in the Indian Constituent Assembly on 25 November 1947, Pandit Nehru said, 'In order to establish our bona fides, we have suggested that when the people are given the chance to decide their future, this should be done under the supervision of an impartial tribunal such as the United Nations Organization. The issue in Kashmir is whether violence and naked force should decide the future or the will of the people.'

5 March 1948

In a statement in the Indian Constituent Assembly on 5 March 1948, Pandit Nehru said, 'Even at the moment of accession, we went out of our way to make a unilateral declaration that we would abide by the will of the people of Kashmir as declared in a plebiscite or referendum. We insisted further that the Government of Kashmir must immediately become a popular government. We have adhered to that position throughout and we are prepared to have a plebiscite with every protection of fair voting and to abide by the decision of the people of Kashmir.'

16 January 1951

In his press conference in London on 16 January 1951, as reported by the daily *Statesman* on 18 January 1951, Pandit Nehru stated, 'India has repeatedly offered to work with the United Nations' reasonable safeguards to enable the people of Kashmir to express their will, and is always ready to do so. We have always, right from the beginning, accepted the idea of the Kashmir people deciding their fate by referendum or plebiscite. In fact, this was our proposal long before the United Nations came into the picture. Ultimately the final decision of the settlement, which must come, has first of all to be made basically by the people of Kashmir, and secondly as between Pakistan and India directly. Of course it must be remembered that we (India and Pakistan) have reached a great deal of agreement already. What I mean is that many basic features have been thrashed out. We all agreed that it is the people of Kashmir who must decide for themselves about their future externally or internally. It is an obvious fact that even without our agreement no country is going to hold on to Kashmir against the will of the Kashmiris.'

6 July 1951

In his report to the All Indian Congress Committee on 6 July 1951, as published in the *Statesman*, New Delhi, on 9 July 1951, Pandit Nehru said, 'Kashmir has been wrongly looked upon as a prize for India or Pakistan. People seem to forget that Kashmir is not a commodity for sale or to be bartered. It has an individual existence and its people must be the final arbiters of their future. It is here today that a struggle is bearing fruit, not in the battlefield but in the minds of men'.

11 September 1951

In a letter dated 11 September 1951 to the UN representative, Pandit Nehru wrote, 'The Government of India not only reaffirms its acceptance of the principle that the question of the continuing accession of the state of Jammu and Kashmir to India shall be decided through the democratic method of a free and impartial plebiscite under the auspices of the United Nations, but is anxious that the conditions necessary for such a plebiscite should be created as quickly as possible.'

2 January 1952

As reported by Amrita Bazar Patrika, Calcutta, on 2 January 1952, while replying to Dr. Mookerji's question in the Indian legislature as to what the Congress Government was going to do about the fact that one-third of Kashmir's territory was still held by Pakistan, Pandit Nehru said, 'It is not the property of either India or Pakistan. It belongs to the Kashmiri people. When Kashmir acceded to India, we made it clear to the leaders of the Kashmiri people that we would ultimately abide by the verdict of their plebiscite. If they tell us to walk out, I will have no hesitation in quitting. We have taken the issue to the United Nations and given our word of honour for a peaceful solution. As a great nation, we cannot go back on it. We have left the question for final solution to the people of Kashmir, and we are determined to abide by their decision.'

7 August 1952

In his statement in the Indian Parliament on 7 August 1952, Pandit Nehru said, 'Let me say clearly that we accept the basic proposition that the future of Kashmir is going to be decided finally by the goodwill and pleasure of her people. The goodwill and pleasure of this parliament is of no importance in this matter, not because this parliament does not have the strength to decide the question of Kashmir but because any kind of imposition would be against the principles that this parliament holds. Kashmir is very close to our minds and hearts, and if by some decree or adverse fortune it ceases to be a part of India, it will be a wrench and a pain and torment for us. If, however, the people of Kashmir do not wish to remain with us, let them go by all means. We will not keep them against their will, however painful it may be to us. I want to stress that it is only the people of Kashmir who can decide the future of Kashmir. We have not merely said that to the United Nations and to the people of Kashmir: it is our conviction, and one that is borne out by the policy that we have pursued, not only in Kashmir but everywhere. Though these five years have meant a lot of trouble and expense, in spite of all we have done we would willingly leave if it were made clear to us that the people of Kashmir wanted us to go. However sad we may feel about leaving we are not going to stay against the wishes of the people. We are not going to impose ourselves on them by the point of the bayonet'.

31 March 1955

In his statement in the Lok Sabha on 31 March 1955, as published in the *Hindustan Times*, New Delhi, on 1 April 1955, Pandit Nehru said, 'Kashmir is perhaps the most difficult of all these problems between India and Pakistan. We should also remember that Kashmir is not a thing to be bandied between India and Pakistan but has a soul of its own and an individuality of its own. Nothing can be done without the goodwill and consent of the people of Kashmir.'

24 January 1957

In a statement in the UN Security Council, while taking part in a debate on Kashmir at the 765th meeting of the Security Council on 24 January 1957, the Indian representative, Mr. Krishna Menon, said, 'So far as we are concerned, there is not one word in the statements that I have made in this council which can be interpreted to mean that we will not honour international obligations. I want to say for the purpose of the record that there is nothing that has been said on behalf of the Government of India which in the slightest degree indicates that the Government of India or the Union of India will dishonour any international obligations it has undertaken.'

Tariq Ali

Afterword: Not Crushed, Merely Ignored

In early July 2010, a Kashmiri lawyer rang me in an agitated
state. Had I heard about the latest tragedies in Kashmir? I had
not. He was stunned. So was I when he told me in detail what
had been taking place there over the previous three weeks. As
far as I had seen, none of the British daily papers or TV news
bulletins had covered the story; after I met with him, I rescued
from my spam box two emails from Kashmir informing me of
the horrors. I was truly shamed. The next day, I scoured the
press again. Nothing. The only story in the *Guardian* from the
paper's Delhi correspondent – it was given a full half-page –
was headlined: 'Model's death brings new claims of dark side
to India's fashion industry'. Accompanying the story was a
fetching photograph of the ill-fated woman. The deaths of
(at that point) eleven young men between the ages of fifteen
and twenty-seven, shot by Indian security forces in Kashmir,
weren't mentioned. Later I discovered that a short report had
appeared in the *New York Times* on 28 June and one the day
after in the *Guardian*; there has been no substantial follow-up.
When it comes to reporting crimes committed by states considered friendly to the West, atrocity fatigue rapidly kicks in. A
few facts eventually percolated through, but they were likely
read in Europe and the US as just another example of Muslims

causing trouble, with the Indian security forces merely doing their duty, if in a high-handed fashion. The failure to report on deaths in Kashmir contrasts strangely with the overheated coverage of even the most minor unrest in Tibet, leave alone Tehran.

On 11 June 2010, the Indian paramilitaries known as the Central Reserve Police Force fired tear-gas canisters at demonstrators, who were themselves protesting about earlier killings. One of the canisters hit seventeen-year-old Tufail Ahmad Mattoo on the head. It blew out his brains. After a photograph was published in the Kashmiri press, thousands defied the police and joined his funeral procession the next day, chanting angry slogans and pledging revenge. The photograph was ignored by India's mainstream press and celebrity trivia–obsessed TV channels. Shortly after that, the Kashmiri capital, Srinagar, and several other towns were put under strict military curfew. Whenever the curfew was lifted, however briefly, young men poured out onto the streets to protest and were greeted with tear gas. In most of the province there was an effective general strike for several weeks. All shops were closed.

An ugly anti-Muslim chauvinism accompanies India's violence. It has been open season on Muslims since 9/11, when the liberation struggle in Kashmir was conveniently subsumed under the War on Terror and Israeli military officers were invited to visit Akhnur military base in the province and advise on counter-terrorism measures. The web site India Defence noted in September 2008, 'Maj-Gen Avi Mizrahi paid an unscheduled visit to the disputed state of Kashmir last week to get an up-close look at the challenges the Indian military faces in its fight against Islamic insurgents. Mizrahi was in India for three days of meetings with the country's military brass and to

discuss a plan the IDF is drafting for Israeli commandos to train
Indian counterterror forces.' Their advice was straightforward:
Do as we do in Palestine, and buy our weapons. In the six years
since 2002, New Delhi had already purchased $5 billion worth
of weaponry from the Israelis, to good effect.

Demonstrations against Indian security forces escalated in
early June 2010, when it was revealed in the extra-alert Kashmiri
press that three young men – Mohammed Shafi, Shahzad
Ahmad Khan and Riyaz Ahmad – had been executed in April
by Indian army officers. A colonel and a major were suspended
from duty, a rare enough event, suggesting that their superiors
knew exactly what had taken place. The colonel claimed that
the young men were separatist militants who had been killed
in an 'encounter' near the Line of Control, the border between
Indian-controlled and Pakistani-controlled Kashmir. This
account is regarded by local police as pure fiction.

A letter from Amnesty International to the Indian prime
minister sent in 2008 listed the country's human rights abuses
in Kashmir and called for an independent inquiry, claiming that
'grave sites are believed to contain the remains of victims of
unlawful killings, enforced disappearances, torture and other
abuses which occurred in the context of armed conflict persist-
ing in the state since 1989. The graves of at least 940 persons
have reportedly been found in 18 villages in Uri district alone.'
A local NGO, the International People's Tribunal on Human
Rights and Justice in Indian-administered Kashmir (IPTK),
states that extrajudicial killings and torture are a commonplace in the valley and that Western institutions don't even
try to do anything about it for fear of damaging relations with
New Delhi. The figures provided by the IPTK are startling. It
claims that the Indian military occupation of Kashmir 'between

1989–2009 has resulted in 70,000+ deaths'. The report disputes claims that these killings are aberrations, but on the contrary are part of the occupation process, considered 'acts of service', and lead to promotion and financial reward (a bounty is paid after claims made by officers are verified). In this dirty and enduring conflict, more than half a million 'military and para-military personnel [more than the number of US soldiers in Iraq and Afghanistan combined] continue to act with impunity to regulate movement, law and order across Kashmir. The Indian state itself, through its legal, political and military actions, has demonstrated the existence of a state of continuing conflict within Indian-administered Jammu and Kashmir.'

Public opinion in India is mute. The parties of the left prefer to avoid the subject for fear that political rivals will question their patriotism. Kashmir is never spoken of, and it has never been allowed to speak. With its Muslim majority, it wasn't permitted a referendum in 1947 to determine which of the two countries, India or Pakistan, it wished to be part of. In 1984, when Indira Gandhi was the Indian prime minister, I asked her why she had not taken advantage of the birth of Bangladesh in 1971 (when Kashmiris had watched with horror how the Pakistan army treated their co-religionists) and allowed a referendum then. She remained silent. I pointed out that even Farooq Abdullah, the chief minister of Kashmir, was convinced that India would win if a democratic election were held. Her face clouded. She said, 'He's completely untrustworthy.' I had to agree, but her refusal to contemplate the Kashmiri self-determination prom-ised by her father, Jawaharlal Nehru, was troubling. These days, the very suggestion seems utopian.

The Abdullah dynasty continues to hold power in Kashmir and is keen to collaborate with New Delhi and enrich itself. I rang a journalist in Srinagar and asked him about the current chief minister, Omar Abdullah, a callow and callous youth whose only claim to office is dynastic. 'Farooq Abdullah', he told me, 'is our Asif Ali Zardari when it comes to corruption. Now he's made his son chief minister so that he can concentrate on managing his various businesses.' The opposition isn't much better. Some Kashmiris, the journalist said, call Mirwaiz Umar Farooq, the effective leader of the opposition, and his cronies 'double agents. That is, they are taking money from Pakistan and India.' He is the twelfth 'mirwaiz', or self-appointed spiritual leader of the Muslims in the Kashmir Valley, and is adept at playing both sides. 'Mirwaiz's security outside his house is provided by the Indian state,' a friend in Srinagar told me. 'His wife is Kashmiri American, he lives very comfortably (without any source of income), and he is engaged in secret talks with India, news of which is constantly leaked. Furthermore, he also makes an annual pilgrimage to Pakistan to keep that channel open as well. He hangs out with "separatists" in Kashmir who are open to being used by both India and Pakistan, for a good price, of course. The Indian authorities do not have to do much to crush Kashmiris while there are people like Mirwaiz. So, all in all, our leadership is working against us. India has always used this to its advantage.'

The Zardari government is silent on the issue of Kashmir and there was little media reaction in Pakistan to the summer 2010 killings. For the ruling elite, Kashmir is just a bargaining counter. 'Give us Afghanistan and you can have Kashmir' is the message currently emanating from the bunker in Islamabad. Zardari, it's worth recalling, is the only Pakistani leader whose effigy has been burned in public in Indian Kashmir (soon after becoming president he seriously downplayed Kashmiri aspirations). The Pakistani president and his ministers are more interested in business deals than in Kashmir. This suits Washington perfectly, since India is regarded as a major ally in the region and the US doesn't want to have to justify its ally's actions in Kashmir. Pakistan's indifference also suggests that Indian allegations that the uprisings in Kashmir were triggered by Pakistan are baseless. Not long after 9/11, Pakistan virtually dismantled the jihadi networks it had set up in Kashmir after the 1989 withdrawal of Soviet troops from Afghanistan. Islamabad, high on the victory in Kabul, had stupidly assumed that it could repeat the trick in Kashmir. Those sent to infiltrate Indian Kashmir were brutal and mindless fanatics who harmed the Kashmiri case for self-determination, though some young people, tired of the patience exhibited by their elders, embraced the jihad, hoping it would bring them freedom. They were wrong.

As Indian politicians stood on the battlements of the Red Fort in Delhi to celebrate Independence Day in August 2008, Kashmiris began a mass campaign of civil disobedience. More than a hundred thousand people marched peacefully to the UN office in Srinagar. They burned effigies, chanted '*Azadi, azadi*' and appealed to India to leave Kashmir. This movement was not crushed. It was merely ignored. Nothing changed. Now a new generation of Kashmiri youth is on the march. They fight, like the young Palestinians, with stones. Many have lost their fear of death; they will not surrender. Ignored by politicians at home, abandoned by Pakistan, they are developing the independence of spirit that comes with isolation, and it will not be easily quelled.

8 July 2010

The dead are:

11 June: Tufail Ahmad Mattoo, 17, killed in tear-gas bombardment in Srinagar.

19 June: Rafiq Ahmad Bangroo, 24, beaten by members of the Central Reserve Police Force near his home in old Srinagar on 12 June, died of his injuries.

20 June: Javed Ahmad Malla, 26, died when mourners, returning from Bangroo's burial, attacked a CRPF bunker, causing its occupants to open fire.

25 June: Shakeel Ganai, 17, and Firdous Khan, 18, killed when the CRPF fired at protesters in Sopore.

27 June: Bilal Ahmad Wani, 22, died following CRPF fire in Sopore.

28 June: Tajamul Bashir, 20, killed in Delina; Tauqeer Rather, 15, killed in Sopore.

29 June: Ishtiyaq Ahmed, 15, Imtiyaz Ahmed Itoo, 17, and Shujaat-ul-Islam, 17, died after being shot by police in southern Anantnag.

5 July: Muzaffar Ahmad Bhat, 17, died in CRPF custody in Srinagar.

6 July: Fayaz Ahmad Wani, 18, shot by the CRPF during Bhat's funeral procession in Srinagar; Yasmeen (Fancy) Jan, 25, the first woman to die, killed when a bullet hit her as she watched events from a window in her house; Abrah Ahmad Khan, 16, killed during protests over Wani's death.

About the Authors

Tariq Ali is a writer and film-maker. He has written more than a dozen books on world history and politics – including *Pirates of the Caribbean, Bush in Babylon, Clash of Fundamentalisms* and *The Obama Syndrome* – as well as the five novels of the Islam Quintet and scripts for the stage and screen. He is an editor of *New Left Review* and lives in London.

Hilal Bhatt is a Kashmiri journalist.

Angana P. Chatterji is a Professor of Social and Cultural Anthropology at California Institute of Integral Studies. Her work focuses on South Asia. She is the co-convenor of the International People's Tribunal on Human Rights and Justice in Indian-administered Kashmir and the author of *Violent Gods: Hindu Nationalism in India's Present*. She lives in California and in India, where she was born.

Habbah Khatun was a sixteenth-century poet. Born a peasant in the village of Chandrahar in Kashmir and known as Zoonie, she became the wife of Sultan Yusuf Shah, ruler of Kashmir, and took the name Habbah Khatun.

Pankaj Mishra is an Indian writer whose work focuses on literature and politics. He is the author of a novel, *The Romantics*, and several non-fiction books, including, most recently, *Temptations of the West: How to Be Modern in India, Pakistan, Tibet and Beyond*. His essays have appeared in many publications, and he is a frequent contributor to the *New York Review of Books* and the *Guardian*.

Arundhati Roy is an Indian writer and activist. She has written screenplays and a novel, *The God of Small Things*, which won the Booker Prize in 1997. Since then she has produced several collections of essays on politics, including, most recently, *Broken Promises*.